# The Official

## ILLUSTRATED GUIDE

TO THE

# SOUTH-EASTERN

## RAILWAY

AND

## ALL ITS BRANCHES.

## BY GEORGE MEASOM.

*Embellished with Forty-four Beautiful Views from Original Drawings.*

LONDON:

W. H. SMITH & SON, LONDON BRIDGE STATION,

BOOKSELLERS TO THE COMPANY,

AND AT ALL THE BOOK-STALLS ON THE LINE.

C. WHITING,]     1853.     [BEAUFORT HOUSE.

First Published 1853

This facsimile edition published
by Countryside Books 1987



COUNTRYSIDE BOOKS
3 Catherine Road
Newbury, Berkshire

ISBN 1 85306 000 3

Produced through MRM (Print Consultants) Ltd., Reading.
Printed in England by J.W. Arrowsmith Ltd., Bristol

# Contents

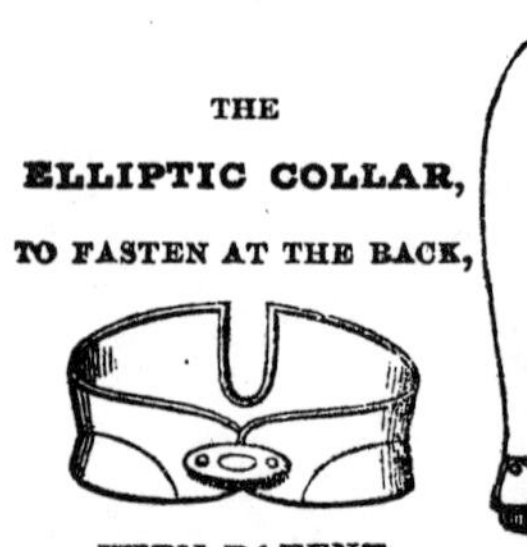


A MOST PERFECT AND EASY FITTING SHIRT, which, by a simple invention of the Patentees, adjusts itself to all movements of the body, both back and front, either walking, sitting, or riding.—Price, including the REGISTERED ELLIPTIC WRISTBAND, 42s. the half-dozen.

The ELLIPTIC COLLAR, quite unique, in all shapes, with PATENT ELASTIC FASTENING, 12s. the dozen.

The PATENT ELASTIC COLLAR FASTENING can be attached to any Collar, opening back or front.

Six sent by Post on receipt of 13 Postage Stamps.

---

### DIRECTIONS FOR SELF-MEASUREMENT.

1. Round the Chest, tight over the Shirt.
2. Round the Waist, tight over the Shirt.
3. Round the Neck, taken about the middle of the Throat.
4. Round the Wrist.
5. The length of Coat Sleeve, from the centre of Back, down the seam of Sleeve to bottom of Cuff.
6. The length of Shirt.
   Say if the Shirts are to open back or front.
   If with Collars attached (3s. the half-dozen extra).

---

PATENTEES,

## COOPER·AND FRYER,

REMOVED NEXT DOOR TO THE

# HAYMARKET THEATRE.

# Introductory Preface.

THE South-Eastern Railway is one of the most important lines in England, opening, in the first place, a direct and rapid communication with the Continent by the way of Folkestone and Dover, and visiting on its road many important stations connected with populous towns and thriving rural districts, affording, also, a rapid means of transit to several favourite watering-places which before its establishment were virtually at a day's distance from London instead of three or four hours; and, lastly, furnishing, with its branches, ready means of access to places in various parts of the southern counties not before traversed by railways, and thus enabling persons to reach other lines without the necessity of going to London to avail themselves of the metropolitan trains.

The original Act of this enterprising Company was obtained in 1836, for the express purpose of constructing a railway from London to Dover, the expenses of which were calculated at 1,400,000*l.*, to be raised in 50*l.* shares; but by subsequent Acts they were authorised to form branch-lines, and for that purpose to make loans and issue new shares, involving for the Maidstone and Isle of Thanet branches an expenditure of 3,564,170*l.*; besides which there has been a further outlay of about 1,800,000*l.*, to complete the Hastings branch and that from Reigate, through Dorking and Guildford, to Reading.

The Greenwich line had been previously constructed, and the Croydon Company had obtained the sanction of Parliament to pass over three miles thereof to New Cross, whence they continued their line seven miles and a half to Croydon. The next ten miles and a quarter, as far as Red Hill, or the Reigate Junction, belonged originally to the South-Eastern and Brighton Companies in joint shares; but the whole has subsequently, as sanctioned by Parliament, been purchased by the South-Eastern Company; so that the whole line, together with the Greenwich line, which it holds on a lease of 999 years, belongs to this Company. More recently, also, besides constructing several branch-lines, the South-Eastern Company has purchased the North-Kent line, thus becoming master of the whole railway-communication for Kent, East Surrey, and a portion of Sussex.

The railway was opened as far as Tunbridge, forty miles from London, on May 26, 1842, from thence to Ashford in the following December, as far as Folkestone in June, 1843, and to Dover in February, 1844. The branch line to Maidstone was opened on Sept. 25 of the same year; that to Hastings, Feb. 1, 1852; and the junction line to Reading in 1849. This railway has seven tunnels on its main line to Dover, and four on its branch lines, some of them of a stupendous character, involving not only great engineering skill, but a vast outlay of capital; besides which, there are numerous embankments, deep cuttings, viaducts, and bridges, which bespeak no ordinary skill.

The South-Eastern Railway, moreover, offers unusual facilities for persons visiting the Continent—for it is *the shortest and most direct route to Paris*, which by its means can be reached three times daily in twelve hours. For this purpose three express trains leave London daily at eight, half-past eleven, and half-past four, independently of the mail train at half-past eight p.m. An express train leaves the London Bridge Terminus every morning specially for the Folkestone tidal-steamer, conveying the passengers direct to the harbour, where a powerful vessel is waiting to receive them, and in two hours afterwards lands them on the quay at Boulogne, without any of the inconveniences of embarking or disembarking in small boats. The times for the departure of these trains are announced in the monthly tables; and this is certainly the shortest, as well as the most comfortable, way of reaching Paris or other parts of the Continent. A morning express train, moreover, leaves London daily at 8.10 a.m., arriving at Dover in time for the South-Eastern and Continental Company's steamer, which sails at 11 a.m., to correspond with the 3 p.m. train from Calais, which arrives in Paris at 10.45 p.m.; besides which there is a night mail train, which, leaving London at 8.30 p.m., reaches Dover at 11.15, in time for the packet, and the train reaches Paris at 9 the following morning. Brussels may be reached by the same medium at 11 a.m., and Cologne at 6.30 p.m., twenty-two hours after leaving London. This route, also, offers immense facilities for reaching distant places on the Continent in an unprecedented short time—as, for instance, Lyons in 30, Marseilles in 46, Hanover in $30\frac{1}{2}$, Bremen in $37\frac{1}{2}$, Hamburgh in 38, Berlin in 41, Dresden in 45, Vienna in 71, and Trieste in 103 hours after leaving the London Bridge Terminus. For all these advantages we owe a heavy debt of gratitude to the South-Eastern Railway Company and its enterprising Directors.

---

## THE FRENCH PORTS.

The luggage of passengers for Belgium or Germany passes in transit over the French territory without any Custom House formality, and is examined at Mouscron, the Belgian frontier station. Those passengers who wish to stay at Calais for a few hours can have their luggage deposited in the Custom House until they leave.

The harbour at Calais is accessible at all times of the tide, the Railway Station is on the Quay, where passengers land from the steamers, and the Police Office, for the examination of passports, is within the Station. An Exchange Office and Refreshment Rooms are also within the Station.

### PASSPORTS.

FRANCE.—English visitors to the ports of France are admitted without passports, but those who intend to proceed to the interior must be provided either with a Passport, or what is termed a "Monthly Pass." Persons who do not intend staying longer than a month in France are recommended to choose the "Monthly Pass," as it is not subject to any *visa* or formality whatever, is in every respect equivalent to a regular Passport, and may be renewed, without charge, for any subsequent journey during a year.

For a longer residence than one month, however, a Passport is required, which is exchanged at the port of landing for a provisional pass, the cost of which is 2 francs, the original passport being sent to Paris, and afterwards to wherever the traveller may have proceeded, when he again receives it in exchange for his provisional pass. On leaving France, Passports must be *viséd* by the British Minister and the Police Authorities. The "Monthly Passes" and Passports are to be had, in London, only at the office of the French Consul-General, 47, King William-street, City, from 11 till 4. The charge for either document is 5s., but several members of the same family and servants can be included in it.

Foreign Office Passports are *viséd* for France at the Consulate, as above. Fee, 4s. 3d.

Passports may be had at Calais, at any hour, from Mr. Morley, the British Vice-Consul. They can also be obtained at Boulogne.

A permit to embark is not required at the French Ports, excep in the case of persons not provided with "Monthly Passes" or Passports.

EXTERIOR OF THE TERMINUS OF THE SOUTH-EASTERN RAILWAYS AT LONDON BRIDGE.

# OFFICIAL
# ILLUSTRATED GUIDE
TO THE

# SOUTH-EASTERN RAILWAY.

## CHAPTER I.

Approaches to the Railway Station—London Bridge, its History and Associations—
St. Saviour's—The Mint—Chaucer and the Tabard Inn—Bermondsey, its Nun-
neries and Tan-yards—Description of the London Bridge Terminus.

THE approach to the South-Eastern Railway Terminus from the north
or London side is, without exception, the most imposing, the busiest,
and the most interesting of all the great roads by which the metropolis
is approached. Proceeding southward from the Bank of England and
the Royal Exchange, which together form the heart or grand centre of
London's commercial life and activity, this line of approach leads
through a noble avenue of large, handsomely-built houses of business,
called King-William street, quite of modern erection, which leads by a
very gentle descent to London Bridge, a place of world-wide celebrity,
that wholly eclipses in importance the far-famed Bridge of Sighs or the
Rialto of Venice—a bridge, however, from which Lord Byron, with his
jaundiced spirit, could see nothing but

> A mighty mass of brick, and smoke, and shipping,
>   Dirty and dusky, but as wide as eye
> Could reach,—with here and there a sail just skipping
>   In sight, then lost amidst the forestry
> Of masts,—a wilderness of steeples peeping
>   On tiptoe through their sea-coal canopy,—
> A huge dun cupola, like a foolscap crown
>   On a fool's head. . . . . . .

The noble poet, surely, could not have reflected on the almost bound-
less wealth and national prosperity, of which such a sight was indica-

tive ; and it surely was but ill-taste to pay St. Paul's, our great modern cathedral, so poor a compliment in connexion with the equally-abused metropolis of our great country.  No reflecting person, indeed, that looks upwards or downwards along the " silent highway " which this noble bridge spans, can fail to recognise in the busy panorama that meets his eye, wheresoever he may turn it, unquestionable signs of industry, activity, and prosperity ; for there is no single " mass of brick " that he beholds but is full of property, and busy hands to manage and distribute it ; the smoke does its bidding in aiding the art of man and sending its products to distant regions ; and the " forestry of masts" tells an unmistakeable tale of trade and commerce that makes London the great emporium of western Europe.

London Bridge has a special claim on our notice from its historical associations ; for it (or rather its predecessor, the old bridge) has been one of London's most familiar monuments for nearly ten centuries. *Now*, it is true, the Thames is crossed here by six noble bridges ; but time was, and not more than a century ago, when London Bridge was the only passage (save by ferries) over this river, the sole free channel of communication between the City and Southwark, the only entrance to London from the south.  The old bridge—and that was the successor of one still more ancient—was built at the close of the twelfth century, from the designs of Peter of Colechurch, who—like William of Wykeham—was a clever architect, as well as a good clergyman ; and it stood about sixty yards below the present structure, close to the church of St. Magnus, near the entrance of the steam-packet quays.  It was formed of nineteen stone arches, besides a large opening in the centre, covered by a drawbridge, with a gatehouse at each end, and a chapel and crypt at the middle, dedicated to St. Thomas (à Becket) of Canterbury, the fashionable martyr-saint of the thirteenth century ; its piers were built on piles, with projecting starlings (perhaps afterwards added), and the bridge was afterwards, by degrees, " covered with houses on both sides, like a continuous street, with void places at certain intervals, and chain-posts along the line, to serve as a retreat for foot-passengers."  It was over this quaint-looking bridge—and its portraiture is still to be seen in the old books about London—that Richard II. passed twice in joyous pomp with his newly-wedded queens ; first with Ann of Bohemia, in 1378, and four years afterwards with Isabella of France,—that Henry V. crossed in triumphant procession after the glorious victory of Agincourt (Oct. 25, 1415), where, with the loss of only 100 men, his army slew 10,000, and captured 14,000 of the French,—that rather more than a century later, gorgeous Wolsey crossed with a numerous and stately retinue on his embassy to France, himself riding " like a cardinal, very sumptuously on a mule trapped with crimson velvet, and having before him his two great crosses of silver, two great pillars of silver, the great seal of England, the cardinal's hat," &c.;—and lastly, to omit all other intermediate instances, it was over this bridge that on May 29, 1660, Charles II. made his solemn entry into London with a gay and splendid cavalcade of the first nobility and gentry of the land, amid universal jubilation for his restoration to the throne of his fathers. The old bridge, also, possesses a melancholy interest, from the fact, that on the top of its gateways at either end the trunkless heads of real or alleged traitors were exposed upon poles; and among these we may mention as the most illustrious, the Scottish warrior William Wallace, who resisted till death the foreign yoke imposed by Edward I.; the Earl of Northumberland, father to the gallant Hotspur, after his defeat in the border-wars; Fisher, Bishop of Rochester; and the celebrated Sir Thomas More, who were both executed in 1535 for refusing to acknowledge the king's supremacy. In fact, during the fifteenth, and throughout the sixteenth century, from thirty to forty heads were generally to be seen at the same time; nor did the custom cease till after the restoration of Charles II., at which time the heads of some of the regicides were here exposed. Meanwhile, in the process of nearly six centuries, time had been making sad havoc with a bridge even originally built on unsound principles, and which had become so oppressed by its own weight of stone, and the rows of houses on each side, as to require from year to year a vast deal of cobbling to keep it together; and at length, in 1757, after much controversy, it was determined to remove the houses and put the bridge in thorough repair. The bridge, however, was incurably defective, from the narrowness of its arches, which not only made the passage through them a matter of difficulty for boats of any kind, but occupied with their buttresses so large an extent of the river as to dam up its waters and prevent the free ingress and egress of the tide. The principal arch was only thirty-six feet wide, the rest varying in size, but all very much more confined;

and hence the resistance offered to so large a body of water by the contraction of the channel to less than one-half its natural breadth produced a rapid or *fall* under the bridge, which it was necessary to *shoot*, an operation only possible at certain periods of the tide, and never unattended with danger; nay, the cause of yearly sacrifices of life. Water-wheels, too, occupied for many years the water-way of some of the smaller arches on the London side of the bridge; and these curious structures, as well as the roar of waters beneath during the ebb-tide, must be quite familiar to the memory of our older readers. In fact, the nuisance of so defective and crazy a structure over a great navigable river like the Thames became so intolerable, that the good citizens of London were at length compelled to abandon this historic relic and form plans for the erection of another and more suitable structure in its stead. The present bridge (which was built from the designs of the Rennies, father and sons) was commenced June 15, 1825, and was publicly opened by William IV. and Queen Adelaide, August 1, 1831. It is built of granite, and is reported to have cost, including the approaches, nearly two millions sterling. It has five elliptical arches, the central one 152, and the others 140 feet span, and is 920 feet long, and 40 feet broad from parapet to parapet.

And now having passed the bridge, and observed the new and handsome clock-tower on the Southwark side, we shall, ere conducting our readers to the station, make a few remarks on a few neighbouring objects of more than usual historic interest; for, as it is well remarked in " Knight's London," " if there be classic ground in London it is this; for, standing on the foot of that bridge which has replaced the venerable piece of antiquity so connected with the local history of Southwark, and looking forwards into the mass of human dwellings beyond, a host of recollections of some of the mightiest intellects of our own, or of any other country, rush upon the mind, in connexion with localities, every one of which might be comprised in a half-circle of a few hundred yards from the river !" First, we see on the right the eastern end of St. Saviour's, formerly the church of the *Priory of St. Mary Overy*, and first erected into a parish church at the dissolution of the monasteries in 1540, when the two parishes of St. Margaret and St. Mary Magdalen were united in one, called *St. Saviour's*, of which this was made the church. Its exterior, though much patched, is well worthy of observation, and the interior presents, after Westminster Abbey, the finest specimens of early English in the metropolis. The choir and Ladye Chapel, however, are the only remnants of the old church; for the nave was pulled down about twenty years ago. The church, too, contains many interesting tombs — especially a canopied monument to the poet Gower (who founded a chantry here), and a marble monument to Launcelot Andrews, Bishop of Winchester; besides which, the parish register bears record to the interment here, in one grave, of the two great dramatic poets, Massinger and Fletcher; of Sir Edward Dyer the poet, who lived in Winchester House, adjoining; and of Edmund Shakspeare (the poet's youngest brother); of Philip Henslowe, the manager of the theatre in which Shakspeare was poet and player too. Beyond the church, too, on the Bankside, was the house of Beaumont and Fletcher, held in common, like their genius; and in the same neighbourhood, close to the river, was the theatre " where Shakspeare nightly trod the stage, and where, from time to time, all the aristocracy of London—whether of rank or intellect— thronged to witness some new production from that wonderful mind." In the street, also, now known as Clink-street, was Shakspeare's residence as late as 1609.

Again, on the opposite side of Wellington-street, facing St. Saviour's, is *St. Thomas's Hospital*, which, though now exclusively devoted to the relief of the sick and diseased poor, was originally founded early in the thirteenth century as a Benedictine monastery, which it continued to be till the dissolution of the religious houses, when it was purchased by the Corporation of London, and applied to its present uses. The church attached to this monastery was pulled down at the close of the seventeenth century, and the present structure in St. Thomas's-street erected on its site. Any account of the " Borough," too, would be very imperfect that did not at least make some reference to *The Mint*, on the west side of Blackman-street—a small poverty-stricken district, that owed its name to a mansion of Brandon, Duke of Suffolk, afterwards converted into a Mint of Coinage by King Henry VIII., but which afterwards attained as disgraceful a notoriety as Whitefriars, for being a sanctuary, or receptacle of broken and desperate men. It is often alluded to by Strype, Pope, Gay, and others; nor was it finally suppressed till the reign of George I.

Far more justly worthy of mention, however, is the *Tabard*, or *Talbot Inn*, on the south side of the Borough High-street, an hostelrie, indeed, of no little celebrity, as having been the place where Chaucer, and the other nine-and-twenty pilgrims to the fashionable shrine of Thomas à Becket, met together to consult with their host on the manner of their journey to Canterbury.  The fact is thus stated by the poet:

> Befel, that in that season, on a day,
> In Southwarke at the Tabard as I lay,
> Readie to wenden on my pilgrimage
> To Canterbury with devout courage,
> At night was come into that hostelrie
> Of sundrie folke by adventure yfall
> In fellowship, and pilgrims were they all,
> That toward Canterbury woulden ride.

No part of the present inn—old and dilapidated as much of it seems—belongs to the age of Chaucer; but a good deal of it dates back as far as the age of Elizabeth.  Its exterior towards the street is simply a narrow, square, dilapidated-looking gateway, with " Talbot Inn" painted over it, having huge, iron-bound, blackened doors, that silently proclaim its great antiquity; but this gateway leads to a yard, which is, perhaps, the most perfect extant pattern of our inns of the olden time.  On either side will be seen a range of brick buildings, and opposite the end of that on the right, the left-hand range is continued by a wooden gallery on the first floor, a part of which faces the entrance from the street.  " Offices, with dwelling-rooms above, occupy the left range as far as the gallery, which is over the stables ; and under the front of the gallery is a waggon-office, which, with its miscellaneous packages lying about, suggests thoughts of the time when as yet road-waggons, properly so called, were unknown, and the carriers with their strings of pack-horses and jingling-bells filled the yard with their bustle and obstreperous notes of preparation for departure."  For further information, however, on this most interesting old hostelrie, we must refer the curious to Mr. Saunders's admirable account of it in " Knight's London," whence this brief sketch has been principally taken.

We must now once more return to the neighbourhood of the Terminus; but ere we finally enter it to commence in earnest on our journey, we will take a turn down the steep incline of Tooley-street and pay a brief visit to Bermondsey, which, though now densely covered with habitations and warehouses, and at an earlier period the site of an abbey of no mean celebrity, was originally, until reclaimed and made useful, a kind of marshy island when the tide was out, and a wide expanse of water when it was in.  Indeed, even at the present day, as Mr. Saunders well remarks, " the very streets have a damp *feel* about them, and in the part known as Jacob's Island, the overhanging houses and the little wooden bridges that span the stream have, notwithstanding their forlorn look, something of a Dutch expression. In short, persons familiar with the history of the place may everywhere see that *Beormund's Ea* still exists, but that it has been embanked and drained—that it has grown populous, busy, commercial." With all its industrial activity, however, Bermondsey has generally but dreary, mouldy-looking streets lined with tumble-down tenements; and it abounds, also, with courts and alleys of the most wretched character, inhabited by an equally miserable and squalid population—a population among which the wretchedness comes more to the surface than in almost any other quarter of the metropolis There appears to have been a religious establishment in Bermondsey even before the Conquest; but the abbey, which afterwards attained such celebrity, was founded by Alwyn Childe, a citizen of London, in 1081, for monks of the Cluniac order (a branch of the Benedictines), and afterwards enriched by King William Rufus with his manor of Bermondsey, by Robert Blewit, Bishop of Lincoln, with the manor of Charlton, and by numerous subsequent benefactors; so that at the time of the Dissolution, this abbey was valued at 474*l*. 14s. The property was then granted to Sir R. Southwell, and by him sold to Sir Thomas Pope, who built a magnificent mansion on the site of the conventual church; but of this, as well as of the monastery itself, all traces have disappeared. The representations, however, in Wilkinson's " Londina Illustrata," prove the abbey to have been a building of considerable architectural merit. The abbey, moreover, is historically of great interest; for in 1154, Henry II., after his coronation, held an important meeting here of his nobles to consult on the general state of the country; and in the reign of Henry III. many of the nobility, having resolved on an expedition to the Holy Land, assembled here to consult on the arrangements of their journey. Bermondsey Abbey, too, gave fitting and willing hospitality to several noble and distinguished visitors; among others, to Katharine, the French consort of the gallant Henry V., who lived here from the king's death till her own, in 1437; and to Elizabeth Woodville, the ill-fated widow of Edward IV., and the mother of the two princes murdered in the Tower by order of Richard III.

As respects modern Bermondsey, it has been observed that there is a greater variety of trades and manufactures carried on in this parish than in any one parish besides throughout the kingdom : and the remark is perfectly true; for while the northern part of the parish along Tooley-street and near the river bank abounds with wharfingers, merchants, rope-makers, ship-chandlers, outfitters, engineers, &c., those portions which lie close to or south of the railway, abound with tan-yards, fell-mongers' warehouses, leather-dressers' shops, and all the other appurtenances of the leather trade, together with wool-warehouses, glue-factories, rope-walks, &c., flanked on the south-east by nursery-grounds and market gardens, that contrast curiously enough with the denser portions of the district. But we have already dwelt too long on the localities neighbouring on the London Bridge Terminus, and we must at once conduct our readers to the Terminus itself.

The approach to the Terminus from London Bridge is by an ascending incline, bounded on the south-west by the grounds of St. Thomas's Hospital, and north-east by a range of shops communicating with Tooley-street. The south-western part is occupied by the booking-offices of the Brighton and South Coast Railway, while the centre, facing the approach-road, forms the Dover office, beyond which is the North Kent booking-office; and north of this again, nearest Tooley-street, is the office of the Greenwich Railway; so that on the same platform, and beneath the same roof, there is all the machinery connected with the arrival and departure traffic of four great lines travelling over at least 500 miles of the southern counties. Every arrangement for the accommodation of travellers is most complete; and perhaps no railway trains leave the metropolis and arrive at their several destinations with more punctuality to the time specified in the tables than those which depart from, or arrive at, this terminus. And, indeed, a busy place it is !

The GREENWICH trade alone employs sixty trains a day in each direction; and then there is a rapidly-increasing traffic on the NORTH KENT LINE, communicating with Woolwich, Gravesend, and Chatham, that employs twenty-two down and eighteen up-trains every day. Again, there is the SOUTH-EASTERN proper, which stretches its iron arms seaward to Whitstable, Margate and Ramsgate, Deal, Dover, Folkestone, Rye, and Hastings, sending in various directions no less than twenty or thirty trains a day. Besides these, we have the SOUTH-COAST RAILWAY, which grasps Hastings at one end, Brighton in the middle, and Portsmouth at the western extremity of its sea-side boundary. And lastly, there is the CROYDON AND EPSOM branch, which has about a

INTERIOR OF TERMINUS AT LONDON BRIDGE (ARRIVAL OF A THROUGH TRAIN).

TERMINI, AS SEEN FROM THE LINE.

dozen stations to accommodate the merchants, professional men, &c., who reside with their families away from the smoke of busy London in the beautiful district of East Surrey. On the whole, therefore, this Terminus may be reckoned as second only to that of the North-Western in the amount of traffic, of which it is the channel; and it is indisputably true, that no other terminus in the metropolis commands, with the same mileage of railway, so many watering-places and other pleasure towns, as the Terminus at London Bridge—from which we are about to take our readers on a tour of inspection down the various lines and branch-lines belonging to the South-Eastern Railway Company.

## CHAPTER II.

The Vicinity: Tiles, Housetops, and Church-steeples — Rotherhithe and the Thames Tunnel—New Cross and Forest Hill—Sydenham and its Crystal Palace —Norwood, its Gipsies and its Spa—Croydon and Addiscombe—Redhill and Reigate.

BEHOLD us now quietly and cozily seated in our carriage; for we have taken good care—and do you, gentle reader and fellow-traveller, always take a similar precaution—*to be in time.* Porters have ceased to roll their trucks, the bell has silenced its iron tongue, the carriage doors have almost ceased to slam-slam; and only the heavy-breathing-engine tells us by its voice that we are not off. But now—the carriages begin to move—throb—throb—throb,—clack—clack, &c., from presto to prestissimo; and we are soon convinced that we are leaving the station and in earnest commencing our journey. We have before observed that the London Bridge Station, and, indeed, the entire *modern* neighbourhood near it, is based on extensive artificial foundations many feet above the natural level of the ground, and therefore, considering that the line passes through what was originally low, marsh land, often overflooded with the tide, it cannot be matter for surprise that the joint line of the London Bridge Railway Companies is carried on arches for the first few miles, until it begins to ascend the very gentle slopes leading towards Lewisham northward,—towards Sydenham more to the south, on the Croydon line. The view, accordingly, from the carriage windows, after leaving the station, is very peculiar, looking over chimney-tops and house-roofs, and into streets, the dimensions and appearance of which tell no very flattering tale as to the prosperity of this district of tan-yards, &c., &c. Yet we must in all fairness except the beautiful building of St. Olave's Grammar School, of which the Rev. Charles Mackenzie is the respected head master. It is of stone, built in the best Tudor style, and really forms quite a feature in this strange neighbourhood, so ill calculated to give foreigners a proper notion of England's wealth and importance. The new Bermondsey Church is a very pretty feature on the south side, and stands on a road that runs by a crossway to Deptford; but beyond this, unless we except the Thames Tunnel (close by old Rotherhithe Church), which

GREENWICH JUNCTION, SOUTH-EASTERN RAILWAY.

was the grandest, though, perhaps, in practice the least useful of the great works projected by the late Sir Isambert Brunel—a work which, finished in spite of difficulties, and dangers, and personal sacrifices that would have daunted any other man, there is little to notice, except the forest of masts belonging to the thousands of vessels of every build, tonnage, and destination that crowd the docks of London, as well on the Surrey side in the New Commercial Docks, as in the larger East and West India Docks on the opposite bank of the river. And just about this part of the line may be noticed on the south side a junction line coming from the Bricklayers' Arms in the Dover-road, which is now used as a depôt for the luggage conveyed along the joint lines.

And now we are rapidly approaching the NEW-CROSS STATION and depôt, whence, pursuing a course quite distinct from that of the Greenwich and North Kent lines, we wend our way rapidly past FOREST-HILL and its pretty suburban villas to the SYDENHAM STATION, so soon to become a favourite resort of all true lovers of what is beautiful in art, science, or nature, by reason of the splendid Crystal Palace now in course of erection at Penge Wood—a building which is to eclipse even the vast Exhibition Building in Hyde Park, and to be, moreover, not ephemeral, but permanent—a lasting monument of what the collective ingenuity of man can bring together in a limited space to represent all that is curious in art or nature belonging to the various countries of Europe and the world at large. *On this subject we shall have to enlarge in another guide book;* and therefore, bidding adieu to all the pleasant scenery and pretty villas about Sydenham, we hasten on to ANERLEY STATION (about eight miles from London Bridge), which is about half a mile south of the pleasant village of Norwood, so long celebrated for its woods and its gipsies; but, alas! the former have been to a great extent cleared to make room for villas, houses, &c., and the latter, scared from their wonted sylvan haunts, have almost wholly disappeared. Norwood, from its elevation, enjoys a fine view of the whole of London from west to east; indeed, no finer panorama of the metropolis can be found than that to be seen from the summit of Westoe Hill. Neither must we forget to mention *Beulah Spa* and its pretty pleasure-garden, long so favourite a resort of the holiday-seeking Londoners, and which under its present proprietor has been greatly improved, and in a measure restored to its pristine consequence as a sort of rural Vauxhall. On—on—again, and we soon pass another station near a road-side inn, yclept " The Jolly Sailors;" and from this part of the line the excursionist commands a good view of the slopes of Upper Norwood crowned with a very pretty church at no great distance from Beulah, the flag of which may be seen floating in the breeze during the fine days of summer. Indeed, the country around is more than usually rich in the beauties of cultivated nature; and in the midst of a district thus delightful the ancient town of CROYDON stands, the station near which we are just approaching, a little after entering our eleventh mile from the London Terminus.

Croydon, which was called *Croin-dene* in Domesday-book, is irregularly built, but consists of a principal street running north and south, with another running eastward, and a third westward to the railway station, and thence to Carshalton, Sutton, and Cheam.  It has a few good modern-built houses, with handsome residences in the suburbs; but, generally speaking, the town has a poor, shabby appearance, little according with the supposed condition of its inhabitants (about 17,000 last year), the burgher-classes of which are mostly supported by the wants of the nobility, gentry, &c., of which numerous families live in the immediate vicinity.  Croydon has a good town-hall and a spacious sessions-house, where the assizes are held alternately with Guildford and Kingston; besides which, it is one of the polling-places at elections for East Surrey.  Croydon had a church annexed to the see of Canterbury long before the Norman Conquest; but of any structure boasting such an antiquity as this, not a trace remains: the present building belongs probably to the fourteenth or fifteenth century, and is of large dimensions, built of flint and stone, and has a lofty square tower, adorned with pinnacles.  It has some good carved work in the interior, with some handsome monuments, especially one in white marble of Archbishop Sheldon (the great benefactor of Oxford), representing that prelate in a recumbent posture; a work, indeed, well worth attention, as having been the production of a London mason in the seventeenth century, a period especially *jejune* in everything that concerns the Fine Arts.  So much for Croydon itself: and now we must take a brief survey of the vicinity, which abounds with handsome seats. Among these, the first place is due to Addington Park, about three miles north-east, the country residence of the Archbishops of Canterbury, though no ancient possession of that see; for although the manor of Croydon has belonged to it since the beginning of the twelfth century, and was not alienated with its old ruined castle, of which we have not spoken till now, this particular property was purchased, only so recently as 1807, for 25,000*l*., by Archbishop Sutton, and enlarged under Dr. Howley, his successor, by the addition of contiguous lands, most of which have been thrown into the park, which is one of the finest in the county, and is beautifully kept up, many parts of it ccm manding delicious views of green, sylvan scenery, both in Kent and Surrey.  The mansion is modern, built near the close of the last century, and subsequently much enlarged by the addition of a chapel.

library, and numerous offices: the rooms, though not large, are well
proportioned, and furnished in the style befitting a churchman; but
no one would suppose that a building of such small architectural pretensions was the country-retreat of the highest clergyman in England,
—the supreme pontiff of our much-beloved Protestant Church. Thanks
be to God, that we now have no false, no wavering primate in these
trying times! May the God of Truth direct the result!

We here present our readers with a very faithful view of Croydon, as
seen from Crowhamhurst,—a picuresque suburb of that town, abound-
ing with pretty villas and gentlemen's seats.

CROYDON, FROM CROWHAMHURST.

About a mile and a half east of Croydon, too, is *Addiscombe*, the well-
known Military College of the East India Company, for the education
of gentlemen-cadets for the engineers, artillery, and infantry in their
service. The estate at one time belonged to William Draper, Esq.,
who married a daughter of the celebrated John Evelyn; and by him
the present mansion was erected from the designs of Sir John Van-
burgh. Lord Grantham and the first Earl of Liverpool occupied it at

the close of the last century; after which the estates devolved on the wife of E. Delmé Radcliffe, Esq., master of the stud to George IV., and by him it was sold in 1809 to its present possessors, by whom the premises have been greatly improved, through the addition of several detached buildings and offices. The present establishment is under the management of an inspector and lieutenant-governor (Major-General Sir C. W. Pasley, and Lieut.-Colonel Abbott), and the instruction of pupils is committed to a staff of five general professors, and several masters in the different branches of military science, including two teachers of the Hindustáni language. The number of pupils averages about 500, who pay a certain yearly sum for their education maintenance, and, if found qualified on examination, are selected for appointment to commissions in the higher grades of the Company's service.

Many of the walks and rides about Croydon are exceedingly beautiful and interesting; and in its vicinity are several handsome seats; as *Haling House*, once the property of the Gages, but now belonging to Ralph Fenwick, Esq.; *Norbury*, the seat of A. K. Barclay, Esq., on an eminence to the west of the London road; *Coombe House; Shirley House*, belonging to the Earl of Eldon; &c. A few remarks, however, must be made respecting *Bedington Park*, which (with one short interval in the sixteenth century) has been the residence of the Carews since the days of Sir Nicholas Carew, keeper of the privy-seal to Edward III., and is now held by Capt. E. Hallowell Carew, R.N., an indirect descendant of the family. Of the original mansion, erected by Sir Francis Carew, and in which he had twice the honour of entertaining Queen Elizabeth, no part remains except the great hall, which is an admirable specimen of the timber-roofed domestic architecture of that period. The present house was erected at the beginning of the last century, and is of brick with stone dressings, comprising a centre and two wings, forming three sides of a square, the fourth side of which is formed by an open iron railing, enclosing the roads of approach. The grounds retain many characteristics of the old school of gardening; among which, towards the east, is a waterfall, supplied by the river Wandle, which intersects the park in its way to the Thames. There is also a spacious canal on the west, derived from the same stream, and ornamented on each side by venerable elms, parallel to which is a noble avenue of stately chesnuts; and near the house, on the north-west, are some remarkably large walnut-trees. The park, which is between three and four miles in circuit, is well wooded, and abounds with deer. Beddington Church, too, which stands within the park, close to the house, is well worth a visit, as containing some fine old monuments, brasses, wood-carvings, &c., of great interest to the antiquarian.

Somewhat more than four miles beyond Croydon is the STOAT'S NEST STATION, from the neighbourhood of which may be seen on an eminence, about two miles to the north-east, *Selsdon Park*, the property of George R. Smith, Esq., who built the present mansion in imitation of the old English style. The centre is occupied by a light cloister of five arches, with a good deal of ornamental bracery-work, &c., and at each extremity are two small turrets, which rise above the embattled parapet running round the house, and command beautiful prospects of the surrounding country. Near here, also, are *Sanderstead Place*, the manorial residence of George Clive, Esq., standing in a finely-timbered park of sixty acres, and *Purley House*, now belonging to E. B. Kemble, Esq., and celebrated in literature as having been the place where the notorious John Horne Tooke wrote his great philological work, oddly enough entitled, "The Diversions of Purley." About three miles further, and the line passes close by the village of *Chipstead*, the church of which presents a good example of the early Norman style, and among its sepulchral memorials is one recording the death, in 1835, of Sir Edward Banks, a man of great original talent as a builder and engineer—one who commenced life as a common labourer, and rose solely by his abilities and good conduct to great wealth and an elevated station—and whose name will ever be memorable, as the builder of our most modern bridges over the Thames—Waterloo, Southwark, and London Bridges. He first became known at Chipstead, about half a century ago, as a labourer on the Merstham Railway, then in course of construction; and taking a great fancy to its retired and picturesque churchyard, he chose it as the depository of his ashes. The parsonage-house, too, deserves a visit; and, indeed, the whole parish is replete with diversified scenery, rural as well as picturesque, including that to be found on the manors of *Shabden* and *Pirbright*, both within its limits. It is not far from this spot that the railway, at a distance of eighteen miles from London, enters the Mers-

tham tunnel, which is exactly a mile long, and cost in cutting about
112,000*l.*, being formed almost entirely by blasting through the lime-

VIEW OF MERSTHAM CHURCH, &C., FROM THE RAIL.

stone, of which there is a vast quantity within the parish of Merstham,
and which was used as the material for building Windsor Castle, and
Henry the Seventh's Chapel in Westminster Abbey.   The chalk, also,
from this part of the Surrey hills burns into excellent lime; and by
way of converting it into a lucrative article of trade, an iron railway
was projected about fifty years ago, to open a communication between
Merstham and the Thames at Wandsworth; the speculation, however,
failed, and only small detached portions of it now remain, that part
from Croydon to Merstham being now the property of the Brighton
Railway Company, and included in their line of permanent way.
Merstham Church is a picturesque old building of the fifteenth century, standing on a knoll above the village, and an object of some
interest on account of its curious font and old monuments; near it is
*Merstham Place,* the seat of Sir William G. H. Jolliffe, an irregular,

but comfortable mansion, surrounded by pleasing, picturesquely-arranged grounds.

MERSTHAM TUNNEL, SOUTH VIEW.—REIGATE JUNCTION STATION.

Behold us now, near the completion of our twenty-first mile from London Bridge, at the REIGATE JUNCTION STATION, near Reigate, where the lines of the South-Eastern and Brighton Companies diverge; that of the latter taking a direction nearly south, while the former sends two lines—one eastward, through Kent, to Canterbury and Dover, the other to Reading, through Guildford, Farnborough, &c. To the first of these lines we shall first introduce our indulgent readers, leaving the latter to the close of the volume; but first, ere we start in continuance of our journey, we must give some description of Reigate, and the notabilities in its immediate neighbourhood.

## CHAPTER III.

Reigate Town, Castle, and Priory—Gatton Park—Godstone—Westerham and General Wolfe—Hever Castle and Anne Boleyn—Penshurst and the Sidneys—South Park and Viscount Hardinge—Sevenokes, Knowle Park, and the Wilderness—Tunbridge Station.

REIGATE, which was anciently called *Church-field*, stands in the valley of the Holmsdale (a branch of the Mole), at the foot of that long range of chalk hills, which, commencing near Farnham on the west, extends across the county from west to east, and enters Kent near Westerham. The history of the manor of Reigate goes regularly back to the reign of William Rufus, who granted it to William, Earl of Warren and Surrey; by whom, probably, or one of its succeeding possessors, the old castle was built, some interesting traces of which may be seen on a hill north of the town. The site is the property of Earl Somers, as lord of the manor; and it comprises an eminence perfectly level at the top, of about fifty feet above the general level of the town, being nearly surrounded also by a dry fosse of considerable breadth and depth. The same Earls of Warren who erected this castle, founded also a monastery, or *priory*, which they endowed for the support of Augustinian monks; and this, with its lands, &c., was granted at the Dissolution to Lord Howard of Effingham (the great admiral) in exchange for the rectory of Tottenham. The mansion now called *Reigate Priory*, which occupies the site of the old monastic precinct, is quite a modern structure, the seat of Earl Somers, consisting of a centre and wings, situated in a park of about seventy acres, a little south of the town. The town itself consists of two streets, running east and west, north and south; and it is on the whole well-built and clean. It has a good market-house and town-hall, as well as a fine church, containing some good old monuments, of various periods. At Red Hill, too, within the parish, there is a handsome district church. There are, also, two or three Dissenting chapels. Reigate has a large market every Tuesday, and monthly cattle fairs. It is a borough by prescription, and has sent two members to the legislature from the 23rd Edward I. to the Reform Act, which deprived it of one of its members, and enlarged the electoral limits. It is also one of the polling-places for the eastern division of Surrey, as well as one of the places for holding quarter-sessions. Its present population is about 4700. In the neighbourhood are several handsome seats and villa residences: among others, *Woodhatch Place* (— Price, Esq.); *Woodhatch Lodge*, the seat of Mrs. Charrington; *Linkfield Lodge*, belonging to Weller Ladbrook, Esq.; *Heath House* (on the manor of Colley), the property of Henry Lainson, Esq., &c. This appears the place, also, to give some account of *Gatton Park*, late the property of Lord Monson, but now of the Countess of Warwick, and which acquired a certain celebrity from its attached manor having been one of the decayed or *rotten* boroughs that were disfranchised by the Reform Act. This privilege seems to have been given with the manor, &c., by Henry VI., to one John Tymperly, in 1449, in return "for certain good and faithful services" rendered to that unhappy monarch. It was afterwards vested in the Crown, and was granted in 1540, by Henry VIII., with other estates, to his divorced wife, Anne of Cleves, in part provision for her maintenance during life. It afterwards passed through a variety of hands, and in sixty years, during the last and present centuries, was no less than nine times in the market, its value being of course greatly increased by its parliamentary privilege, now happily for ever removed. The present mansion is an extensive edifice, owing most of its attractions to the late Lord Monson, who greatly improved and enlarged it; and the principal front commands an extensive range of scenery, including a small lake, with banks fringed with fine woods and rich foliage. The park is of great extent, much diversified in level, and most abundantly timbered, especially with elms and beeches, of stately and luxuriant growth. It contains also the fine old church of Gatton, which was entirely renovated in the most correct taste by Lord Monson. It consists of a nave, chancel, and one transept, having also a small tower and shingled spire. The interior is beautifully fitted up with elaborate carvings, oaken stalls, and other ornamental work, procured chiefly in Flanders, and the windows are enriched with stained and painted glass of high merit. At the west of the nave, also, is a Gothic screen, obtained from an English church, after the more than asinine stupidity of a booby churchwarden had consigned it to destruction: it is a fine specimen of open carved work. At the same end, too, raised on a plinth and step, is a very curious octagonal font. In the churchyard is a simple stone mausoleum, in which the late Lord Monson's remains were

deposited, in June, 1841.  This estate, however, must not be con-
founded with the manor of *Upper Gatton*, which belongs to John
Currie, Esq., and comprises a handsome modern mansion, standing on
the high ground towards Chipstead, and surrounded by a park of about
one hundred acres.

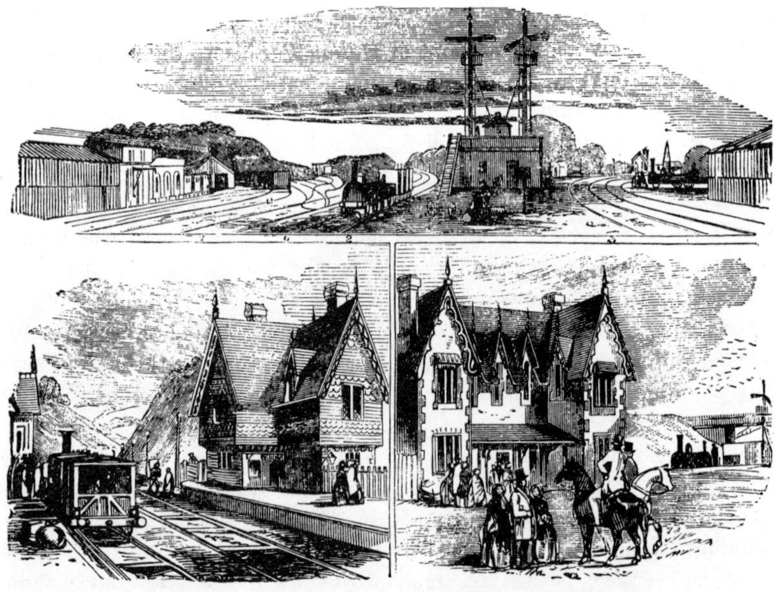

**REIGATE JUNCTION.**

1. South-Eastern Line (Dover Line).    3. South-Eastern (Reading Branch).
2. Brighton Line.    4. Cutting for Sand and Ballast.

**BETCHWORTH STATION.**        **DORKING STATION.**

Our local gossip, however, has detained our fellow-travellers too long
at the Junction terminus; so we must put on additional steam, and
rattle away with express speed to Tunbridge, the next principal station, yet not forgetting to note in our way all that is worthy of observation in this part of Kent.  First, we may mention the pretty village
of *Nutfield*, on the southern edge of the chalk range overlooking the
South Downs, and further on, *Bletchingly*, on the same high ground as
the former, a place of considerable antiquity, that once boasted of a
castle erected soon after the Conquest, but destroyed about the middle
of the thirteenth century; not far from this village are a Roman bath

and other remains of that period when Britain was under the Roman dominion. It is in this part of its course, also, not more than half a mile from the village, that the railway passes through *Bletchingly tunnel*, 1080 yards in length, cut through chalk and limestone rocks; soon after leaving which it reaches the GODSTONE STATION, somewhat more than two miles south of the village whence it derives its name. Here *Flower Hall* and *Marden Park* present a beautiful sylvan appearance of great interest to the lovers of nature. At the extremity of the park, too, near Godstone, is a square building called the *Castle*, the history of which is little known, but remarkable for a wooden tower surmounted by a flag-staff; the windows command delightful and extensive views of the whole country southward, including Sussex and the Weald of Kent. At no great distance, too, is *Tandridge Hall*, lately renovated in exceedingly good taste, and having a fine appearance. Many of the rooms are ancient, and the building is on the whole a remarkably good specimen of domestic Tudor architecture. The parish of Tandridge once boasted of a priory of Augustine monks, founded in the reign of Richard I.; but all the trace left of it is its name, given to a farm-house. The church, however, is an object well worth attention, beautifully situated on a knoll close to a gigantic yew-tree; and it has been within the last few years skilfully renovated, so that few country churches in the neighbourhood, except Gatton, can be found to compete with it. The visitor of Tandridge, too, will be much pleased, if he has leisure, by walking over to *Limpsfield*, a rural, picturesque village, about two miles distant, with a very pretty church.

Five miles further bring us to the EDENBRIDGE STATION, thirty-two miles from the London Terminus, and the first station on entering Kent, being an important station, also, as leading and having conveyances to different towns and villages in the neighbourhood. The adjoining village owes its name to a little stream, the Eden, one of the tributaries of the Medway, and it has a quaint old church at its eastern end. About four miles to the north-east is *Westerham*, a market town just on the eastern border of Surrey, the manor of which was anciently in the possession of the Camville family, but reverted to the Crown at the close of the thirteenth century, when Edward I. granted it, with Edenbridge, to the Abbot of Westminster for the performance of masses for the repose of the soul of his beloved Queen Eleanor. The church is a large and rather handsome building, containing a variety of interesting tombs and brasses, especially a cenotaph in memory of General Wolfe, the conqueror of Quebec, who died there in the arms of victory, Sept. 13, 1759, aged only thirty-two, after a brief career of brilliance unequalled in our military annals. South of the line, not far from Edenbridge, we may reach an object of very great historical interest, and which, although now a ruin, is in so perfect a state as to be well worth a lengthened visit; we allude to *Hever Castle*, the seat of the Boleyns, and the scene of many a happy day's courtship, when Henry VIII. was wooing the beautiful but ill-fated Anne Boleyn, whom that cruel monarch sacrificed without remorse when his sated passion longed for some new object. It was built by the Hever family, from whom it passed to the Cobhams, who, after retaining it nearly two centuries, sold it in 1458 to Sir Geoffry Boleyn, a wealthy mercer of London, who was the grandfather of Sir Thomas Boleyn, afterwards Viscount Rochford and Earl of Wiltshire and Ormonde, the father of the unhappy queen, Anne. After his death, the unprincipled monarch seized the estate in right of his murdered wife, and bestowed it, with other manors, in part provision for his divorced queen, Anne of Cleves, after whose death the castle and property reverted to the Crown. It subsequently came into the possession of the Waldo family (descendants from the great Peter Waldo, of Lyons, who in 1170 first publicly opposed the corruptions of the Church of Rome), and it is now the property of Ralph Waldo, Esq. The castle is a fine, venerable pile, and is surrounded by a moat supplied with water from the Eden, and crossed by a drawbridge. The entrance-gateway, consisting of a large centre flanked by round towers, is embattled and defended by a portcullis; it leads to the inner buildings, which are formed round a quadrangle. The great hall still exhibits traces of its pristine grandeur, when the Boleyns were court favourites, and a monarch visited it to woo its mistress; and the great staircase, which still has several fine windows of painted glass, communicates with various apartments, wainscoted with small oaken panels, and a long gallery with a curiously ornamented ceiling in stucco. Opening into the gallery, too, is a small apartment, which is said to have been occasionally used as a council-chamber by Henry VIII., and at its upper end is a part of the floor which lifts up and discloses a narrow, gloomy descent leading to the moat outside the castle. *Hever Church*, likewise, is well worth a visit, as containing a stately black marble tomb of the Earl of Wiltshire, Anne's father, and some yet more ancient memorials of the Cobhams of Sterborough, the ancient lords of the manor. Near Hever, too, is the lovely village of *Chiddingstone*, rich to profusion in the gabled architecture of the sixteenth century, a pretty specimen of which is exhibited by its unpretending road-side hostelry, the landlord of which is ever anxious to furnish every comfort to the wayworn traveller or pleasure-seeking excursionist. It is one of the prettiest of the many pretty retired villages so frequent in the Weald of Kent, and never seen without communicating ideas of rural happiness and repose.

Another run of five miles through a lovely country brings us to the PENSHURST STATION, an intermediate station, thirty-seven miles from London and two from *Penshurst Castle*, the far-famed seat of the Sidneys, from the reign of Edward VI., by whom it was given, " with the manours, lands, and appurtenaynces therunto belonginge, vnto his trvstye and wel-beloved servant, Syr William Sydney, Knight Banneret," one of the heroic warriors at Flodden Field. The castle, which stands near the south-west corner of a noble park of considerable extent and much diversified surface, is a large castellated structure formed into quadrangles, and exhibiting the various styles of two or three successive centuries. The old hall, with its noble timber roof, belongs to an age long prior to the proprietorship of the Sidneys; the steps in some parts of the mansion are mere rude, solid blocks of oak, and the floors of many of the apartments are formed of huge planks of the same wood, that seem to have been hewn out with the adze than cut by the saw and polished by the plane; whereas other parts exhibit the marks of architectural periods considerably nearer our own day—some, indeed, within the present century, at the time of the last renovation. The state-rooms are of noble dimensions, splendidly furnished, and hung with a great number of valuable historical and family pictures—especially portraits of the Sidneys and Dudleys, some of which are by Holbein—portraits, the very sight of which must call up reminiscences of that great family, whose most distinguished member was, *facile princeps*, the elegant, gallant, and accomplished man of his time ; a person, moreover, of such super-eminent virtues, that without titles, place, court, favour, or other generally acknowledged claims to respect, " he had homage from all eyes, commanded attention from every ear, and won the affection of all hearts." We allude to SIR PHILIP SIDNEY, the son-in-law of Sir Francis Walsingham, and the author of the " Arcadia," one of the earliest and best specimens (partly in prose, part verse) of the heroic romance.  His son Robert was created Lord de L'Isle and Earl of Leicester by James I.; and one of the second earl's sons was the celebrated ALGERNON SIDNEY, the author of the "Oceana," the brother of Waller's "Sacharissa," and the murdered victim, in 1683 (owing to his advocacy of constitutional principles), of the unjust and sanguinary Judge Jeffreys.  The present owner, who inherited from the female line, but adopted the name of Sidney, married one of the Misses Fitzclarence, daughters of the celebrated Mrs. Jordan, and was created Lord de L'Isle by our late King, William IV.  The church is worthy of notice, not only on account of its intrinsic architectural beauties, but for the many monuments it contains of the various possessors of Penshurst (or, as it was anciently called, *Pencester*), including not only the Sidneys, but the Pencesters, the original grantees the Columbers, the Pulteneys, and the Devereux.

The same neighbourhood, also, is rendered illustrious by an estate, *South Park* (about two miles south), the demesne of LORD VISCOUNT HARDINGE, the only fit successor to his great tutor in warfare, the late Duke of Wellington, the greatest of our British heroes—a man whose praise can be better felt in the heart than expressed in volumes of eulogy. Lord Hardinge has considerably added to the estate by subsequent purchases; besides which, with that taste for domestic architecture which for many years has furnished amusement for his leisure hours, his lordship has made many improvements in the mansion.  The friend of poor Sir John Moore, the campaigner of the Peninsula, the Brigadier-General of the Prussian troops under Blucher in the campaign of Waterloo (where he lost his left hand), and the victorious commander (in connexion with Lord Gough) on the fields of Ferooseshah and Sobraon, needs no eulogium in a slight sketch like the present; but we may be allowed to add, that perhaps there was no Governor-General of India, since the formation of the Company, who ever attended so much to the educational and religious interests of British India, as this great officer; and this, after all, will prove his great claim to the respect of future and more peaceful generations; for though energetic, untiring, and unflinching in action, if needed, no one, we believe, more repudiates the necessity of war than the present commander-in-chief.

A few miles north of the line near this point—one of great historical interest, and a place better noticed here than in connexion with Tunbridge—we allude, of course, to *Sevenokes*, and all its beautiful associations of park-scenery, well worthy of a leisurely two days' visit; for who that has heard of Sevenokes has not heard the praises of Knole Park, the seat of the Sackvilles, and of the Wilderness hard by, belonging to the Marquis of Camden?

*Knole Park* encloses an area of more than 1600 acres, and is nearly six miles in circumference, of undulating surface, most judiciously planted, and abundantly timbered with spreading elms, stately beeches, and venerable oaks, some of which have attained enormous size; besides which there are many parts of it that command delicious prospects of secluded woodland scenery, as well as of the more distant country, including the greater part of West Kent, with parts of Sussex and Hampshire. The mansion, which was begun by the Bigods, Earls of Norfolk, late in the fourteenth, and completed in the debased Elizabethan style—probably by the first Earl of Dorset—at the beginning of the seventeenth century, forms a spacious quadrangle, with smaller ones behind it, covering altogether more than five acres of ground; and it is built chiefly in the castellated style, with numerous square towers, and two embattled gateways or tower-portals—one leading to the outer, the other to the inner, quadrangle. The great hall, which is nearly eighty feet long by thirty in breadth, and about twenty-seven feet high, has a raised dais or platform at its upper end, and at the opposite extremity a richly carved screen, surmounted by a music gallery, whence, no doubt, hautboy and dulcimer once sent melodious welcome to the numerous and quickly-succeeding guests of the hospitable Sackvilles. Many of the apartments are gorgeously furnished, and decorated with elaborate carved work; but, after all, the historical portraits and other pictures form the chief attraction for a visitor of cultivated taste, for they include several paintings by Holbein of great historical interest, as well as others, more recently added, by Titian, Corregio, Vandyke, Rembrandt, Sir J. Reynolds, &c. There are likewise some fine specimens of paintings on glass, and a fine collection of busts, principally collected in Italy by the last Duke of Dorset, on whose death, in 1829, the property came into the possession of the Countess of Plymouth, who, in 1839, married the Earl of Amherst, its present occupant.

The *Wilderness* lies in a valley within the parish of Seale, about two miles west of Sevenokes. The house, though spacious, has few archi-

tectural pretensions, but it has a beautiful verdant lawn in front, overlooking the park, which is well stocked with deer, and behind it
beautiful and well-kept gardens well worth a visit.  The park-drives,
too, command extensive and fine prospects over the neighbouring
country.   One of the park gates opens on the turnpike-road close to the
village of Riverhead, and not far from the bottom of Madamscourt Hill,
of gone-by celebrity for highway robberies and stage-coach accidents.

*Sevenokes* itself is a very pretty market town, standing on an eminence, and consisting chiefly of a single street in the line of the Tun-
bridge-road ; and it has a handsome church and well-supported national
schools, besides a grammar school, founded early in the fifteenth century by Sir W. Sevenokes, a native of the town, and afterwards char-
tered by Queen Elizabeth.  To those, however, who knew the place in
the bustling days of posting and coaching, it must now appear extremely dull, and the inhabitants painfully feel the difference, though
they still enjoy a considerable retail trade, owing to the great numbers
of distinguished and wealthy landholders residing in its immediate
neighbourhood.  Sevenokes at the late census was found to have 5780
inhabitants.

TUNBRIDGE STATION AND CHURCH.

# CHAPTER IV.

Tunbridge : its School, Castle, and Priory—Summerhill—Paddock-Wood Station —Wateringbury—Barham Court—Maidstone, the Mote, and Lord Romney— Malling Abbey and Allington Castle.

ON—on now four miles further; and behold us approaching the TUNBRIDGE STATION (a little south of the town of that name), a principal station, and a large one too—being also the *point de départ* for that branch of the South-Eastern Railway (to be hereafter described) which leads through Tunbridge to Hastings and the south coast. The buildings are very extensive, covering nearly twelve acres of ground; for at one time it was a depôt as well as a station, and there is every convenience for the great traffic of a large town and an important junction.

The few minutes of necessary delay here will permit us to take a brief survey of TUNBRIDGE, which may be described as consisting of one handsome, clean, and gas-lit main street, running north and south in the line of the old coach road nearly three-quarters of a mile long, with several minor streets branching from it, including some pretty terraces, squares, &c., in the outskirts; and at the southern end of the town runs the river Medway, divided into five streams, which are crossed by a corresponding number of bridges. The principal bridge, which crosses the southernmost of these channels, was built in 1775; and close to it is the great manufactory of wooden boxes, toys, &c., so well known as *Tunbridge ware,* and which has been conducted by the Wise family for upwards of a century. The church is an elegant stone structure with a square tower, of modern erection, but containing some interesting monuments, especially one sculptured by Roubillac; the incumbent is the Rev. Sir Charles Hardinge, Bart., of Great Bounds Park, Bidborough, the eldest brother of the gallant Viscount Hardinge, our present commander-in-chief. The town has also three or four Dissenting chapels; and there is a good national school. The great glory of Tunbridge, however, is its grammar school, which has for many years enjoyed high repute as a classical seminary : it was founded in 1554 by Sir Andrew Judd, alderman of London, and is under the government of the Skinners' Company, who annually come down to examine the scholars. The revenues now exceed 4500*l.* a year, and the head master (now the Rev. Dr. Welldon) receives a salary of 500*l.*, with a handsome residence. All boys resident within ten miles of Tunbridge are admissible to the foundation; besides which, there are others who pay a small quarterage. Tunbridge school has also considerable university endowments, viz., a fellowship at St. John's, Oxford; a scholarship of 20*l.* a year at Brasenose, Oxford; sixteen open exhibitions of 100*l.* per annum; two exhibitions at Jesus College, Cambridge, of 75*l.*; and ten minor exhibitions; all of which are fairly distributed according to merit. The present number of scholars is about 120, of whom about 40 are on the foundation. The buildings, also, are very handsome, and well worthy of so important an institution. Tunbridge, moreover, possesses no trifling interest for the antiquary, owing to the ruins of its castle and priory. The former of these, which is supposed to have been erected by Richard, Earl of Clare, in the eleventh century, at one time enclosed six acres of ground, and was surrounded by three moats; but little now remains of it except the keep, small portions of the walls, and an inner gateway, said to be the finest extant specimen of Norman architecture in this country. This fortress, however, is historically extremely interesting, as having been besieged by William Rufus in his contests with his brother of Normandy. It was captured by King John in his struggle with the barons; and in the reign of Henry III., when it was besieged by his son Prince Edward (afterwards Edward I.), the town was burnt by the garrison to check the approach of the royal forces. It devolved to the Crown in the reign of Edward II., and subsequently became the property of the Earls of Stafford, afterwards Dukes of Buckingham, until the attainder of the last duke of that family in 1521, when it again reverted to the Crown. Elizabeth gave it to her kinsman Lord Hunsdon, from whom it passed to the Berkeleys, and from them to the Vanlores, the last of whom died without male heirs in the seventeenth century. The Priory was founded in the middle of the twelfth century for black canons by Clare, the first Earl of Hertford, and was suppressed in 1526 among the smaller monasteries at the instigation of Cardinal Wolsey, to whom it was granted by Henry VIII., in order to enlarge the endowment of his college at Oxford. The buildings seem from their foundations to be extensive;

but of the fabric itself scarce a trace remains, except the chapel and great hall, which have been turned into barns.  Up and down the town, too, the antiquarian visitor will find some quaint-looking old houses, which undoubtedly were of some consequence in former times, especially one near the town-hall (now, we believe, the *Chequers* public-house), which bears the strongest marks of antiquity.  Tunbridge has a well-supported literary institution, a mechanics' institute, a joint-stock bank, savings bank, and two very good inns; besides which it is the seat of a county court, a polling place for West Kent, and the centre of a large poor-law union, the workhouse of which is at the neighbouring village of Pembury.  The population of the town at the late census amounted to 16,540, the greater part of whom depend on retail trade for the supply of the neighbourhood, though there are many independent families resident here for the purpose of enjoying the great educational advantages furnished by the grammar school.  The neighbourhood abounds with fine seats, pretty villas, &c.; and perhaps there are few towns in England the environs of which furnish such beautiful walks and drives as Tunbridge.

TUNBRIDGE, FROM THE RAILWAY BRIDGE.

The train is again in motion, and we soon pass on our right, or south side, the beautiful park of *Summerhill*, now the property of Baron de Goldsmidt, the wealthy Jew contractor, and soon afterwards the small, and nearly united villages of Tudeley and Capel; soon after which we complete our forty-sixth mile, and dash into the PADDOCK-WOOD STATION, whence the Maidstone line branches off northward, following pretty closely the course of the Medway to that town. Having now reached a junction station—already of no small importance, and which promises to be more important still, when the contemplated line between Rochester and Maidstone, uniting the North Kent and South-Eastern railways,—we shall now, for a short time, delay our journey along the main line, in order to give a brief description of the branch line to Maidstone. Kent has scarcely any district more beautiful or more productive than this part of the valley of the Medway, close to which the line runs for three-fourths of its course; for in the course of ten short miles it traverses a fine undulating country, rich with orchards, hop-grounds, and corn-fields, and interspersed with pretty villas and aristocrat-looking mansions in noble, finely-timbered parks. The line runs north-north-east for the first two or three miles, and crosses the Medway near Twyford Bridge, just before reaching the YALDING STATION, beyond which it runs along the left bank of that river all the way to Maidstone. The village of Yalding stands on the little river Beult, a little above its confluence with the Medway; but it possesses few features of interest. Beyond it are the fine heights of Yalding Downs and Barnes Hill. About a mile to the left of the station is *Roydon Hall*, the property of W. Cooke, Esq., in the parish of East Peckham; and not far distant are *Nettlested* and *Mereworth Place*—the former, very interesting to the antiquarian, as exhibiting the remains of a seat belonging to the formerly distinguished, but now extinct, family of the "Pimpes;" the latter, a handsome modern mansion of Palladian architecture, built by the eighth Earl of Westmoreland, in the midst of a beautiful, well-wooded park, commanding extensive views of all the surrounding country. It now belongs to the Baroness le Despencer. Two miles further, and we reach the WATERINGBURY STATION, close to the beautiful village of that name, which owes much of its simple elegance to the late Alderman Lucas (whose family hold estates here), by whom most of the houses were rebuilt in the old rustic character; in fact, it is quite a model village, of which its simple inhabitants are not a little proud, and cultivate their gardens accordingly, with a care almost equal to that bestowed on pleasure-grounds of greater extent and pretensions. Close to it is *Wateringbury Place*, an extensive demesne, originally belonging to the ancient family of Waterbury, whence it passed to the Seybournes, and on default of heirs escheated to the Crown; after which, it was given by Edward III. to a monastery of Cistercians, who held it till the Dissolution. It has been in the possession of the "Style" family since the reign of James I., and is now held by Sir Thomas Style, Bart. The present mansion was built in the reign of Queen Anne, on the site of an older one that was surrounded by a moat. Wateringbury has a handsome Gothic church, with some fine monuments of the Style family. Another mile, and we pass the pretty village of *Teston*, which has a bridge over the Medway—here remarkably picturesque—adding not a little to the charms of the richly-cultivated scenery on its banks; adjoining is the demesne of *Barham Court*, which has a park of some 500 acres, and a handsome modern mansion, belonging to the Earl of Gainsborough, whose son is the rector of the parish. The next objects for notice are on the right side both of the river and railway; namely, *West* and *East Farleigh*, both of them exceedingly pretty, with several elegant seats and villas; the church being in the latter—and a very picturesque country church it is—with a square ivy-clad tower, surmounted by a quaint-looking octagonal steeple—the whole well kept, and the interior well worthy of a visit. The living is of considerable value, and till lately was held by the Rev. J. T. Wilberforce, who, two years ago, joined the Church of Rome. It was, on his vacation of it (greatly to the honour of Lord Chancellor Truro), conferred on the Rev. Thomas Watson, for many years a most laborious London curate. The FARLEIGH STATION is near the old bridge over the Medway, and about a quarter of a mile from the village, which, rising as it does rather sharply from the river-bank, and being thickly interspersed with hop-grounds and orchards, has a very pleasant appearance from the railway. Two miles more bring us, at length, to the MAIDSTONE TERMINUS, which has a station, if not of any striking architectural character, at any rate fully adequate to the great traffic belonging to so important a town as that now about to be described.

D

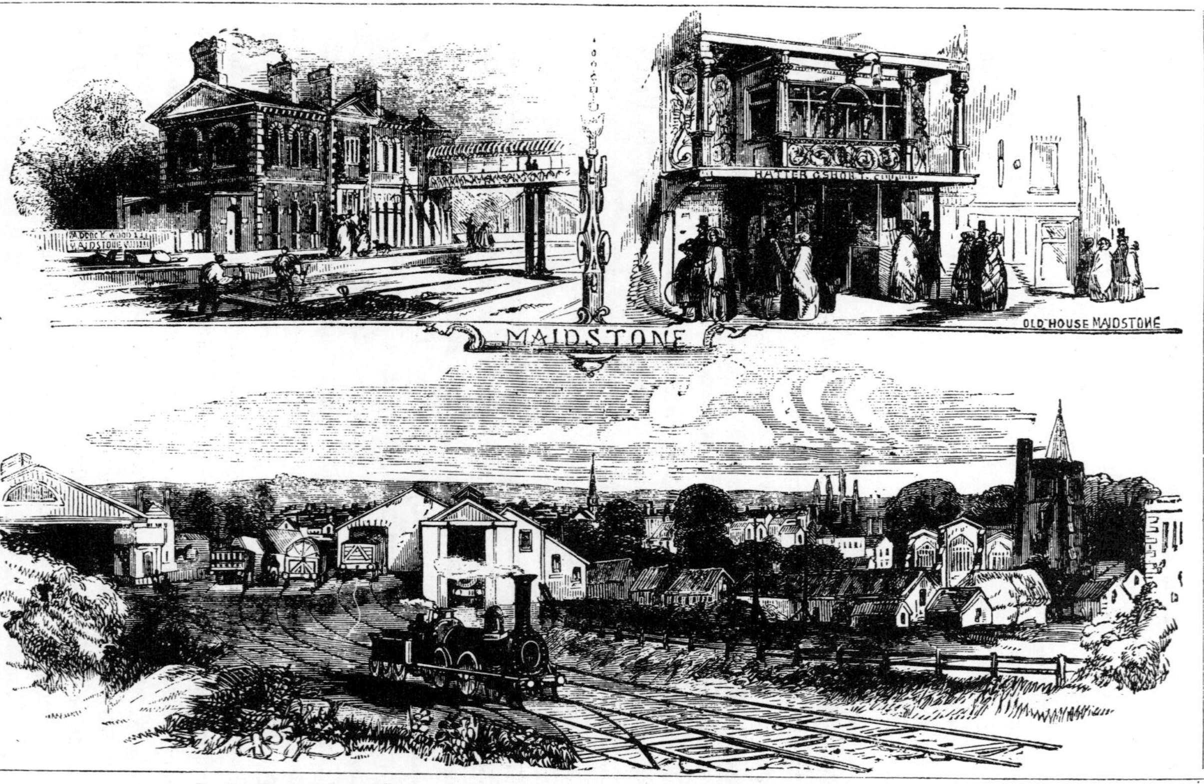


PADDOCK-WOOD STATION.—OLD HOUSE, AT MAIDSTONE.—MAIDSTONE FROM THE LINE.

MAIDSTONE (which in "Domesday Book" is termed *Medestane*) stands on sloping ground, partly on the right, but 'principally on the left bank of the river, which is here crossed by an old stone bridge of five arches. It consists principally of two leading streets, crossing each other at right angles, and is, on the whole, clean, respectably paved, lighted with gas, and abundantly supplied with water from two or three neighbouring reservoirs. Maidstone is a county and assize town; and hence it is a place of no small traffic, has a well-built town-hall, some handsome commercial rooms opposite, used as a corn-exchange, and a good market-place. It is also a military depôt, and has on the right river-bank extensive barracks, with accommodation for about 600 men, and stabling for 300 horses; the whole establish-ment being regulated by a staff of permanent officers. On the Rochester road is the county prison (used also by the borough), which covers fourteen acres of ground, has accommodation for about 350 prisoners, and cost in its erection about 200,000*l*. The front towards the road is used for offices, and purposes connected with the assizes, for which there are two handsome courts. Maidstone has, also, a well-regulated county lunatic asylum, a small infirmary for West Kent, and an ex-tensive union-workhouse for ten parishes, besides numerous almshouses and other charities, bequeathed for the support of the town-poor. As respects ecclesiastical affairs, the manor of Maidstone belonged, from the Conquest downward to the year 1538, to the see of Canterbury; when Cranmer surrendered it to Henry VIII.; and the archbishops resided here during the fourteenth and fifteenth centuries. Of this old palace there are still very interesting remains; now, we believe, forming two private residences. There are rather extensive remains, likewise, of a pilgrims' college, founded by the great Archbishop Courtenay at the close of the fourteenth century—no doubt for the accommodation of the Canterbury-seeking devotees—the funds of which were converted to the more useful purpose of founding a free grammar-school, which still exists under the able management of the Rev. J. Spurgin, and has two exhibitions to University College, Oxford. The antiquarian, also, will find some small remains of an ancient church—St. Faith's—which after the Reformation was used by the Walloons refugees, who retired during the religious persecutions of the sanguinary Duke of Alva, and introduced here the manufacture of linen-thread; of which, however, or the emigrants, not a trace remains! The parish church, which stands near the south-west extremity of the town, is one of the largest in Kent, having been built at different periods—chiefly in the early English style, and very beautifully restored a few years ago: the stalls still existing in the chancel prove it to have been once collegiate. The living is valued at 960*l.* a year, and is in the gift of the Earl of Romney, the lord of the manor of Maidstone. There are, also, three modern district churches within the parish, one of which, Trinity Church, cost 13,000*l.*, and has accommodation for about 2000 persons. Maidstone has, also, eight or nine Dissenting chapels, to all of which, as well as the churches, well-conducted Sunday-schools are attached, furnishing religious instruction to upwards of 2000 children. The grammar-school has been already mentioned; but, in addition to this, in 1846 a diocesan school was opened for agricultural and commercial instruction, under the patronage of the archbishop and clergy, together with an attached model school, both of which, we believe, are prospering. As for minor free-schools (blue and grey coat, &c.), Maidstone is rich in them; and neither the young nor the aged poor, really belonging to the town, need fear of getting support. The principal places of amusement or literary resort, are the Assembly and Music Rooms, opposite the barracks, the Literary and Scientific institution, and the Mechanics' Institute. The theatre is open only occasionally, and little patronised, except by the military. That Maidstone is an assize town has already been mentioned; besides which, quarter and petty sessions, a court of record, and county court are held, so that a good deal of law business is centred here. Neither is it without manufactures of some importance; for the first quality drawing-papers in this country are made at Whatman's (now Balston's) factory, Maidstone Mills, which employ nearly 900 hands: in fact, Whatman's papers are known by artists all over the world. The town has, likewise, some manufactures of felt, coarse blankets, hop-bagging and sacking, employing, perhaps, 250 persons; independently of which, it has a thriving retail trade, and a considerable river traffic, much increased by recent improvements in the Medway navigation. It thus easily exchanges its hops and rag-stone (from quarries hard by) for the coal, timber, and iron, required for home consumption; but we suspect that the river dues have been much decreased since the establishment of this branch of the South-Eastern Railway. The market for corn—and for hops during the season—is on Thursday; for provisions on Saturday; and there are large monthly cattle fairs.

Maidstone is both a municipal and parliamentary borough, being governed by a mayor, five other aldermen, and eighteen councillors, with the privilege of a court of record; and it has about 460 registered electors. The town contains three good hotels and posting-houses, two banks (one, Mercer and Randall's), and two newspapers, one the *Maidstone Gazette*, the other the *Maidstone Journal and Kentish Advertiser*. Ere quitting Maidstone, too, we must call our fellow-traveller's attention to a fine old specimen of domestic architecture in Bank-street, in the possession of Mr. Short, a well-known hatter of that town: —a view of it is shown in our engraving. And now, before we return to the main line, we must devote a few sentences about its beautiful vicinage, 4500 acres of which are planted with hops, and during the summer season exhibit, with their poles, all the pleasing features of a French or German vineyard. Perhaps the most celebrated of all places near Maidstone is *Penenden Heath*, a great place for *shire-gemotes*, or county gatherings, even before the Conquest, and still used for great county meetings, as well as to hang capital criminals tried at Maidstone. A building, or hustings, is erected there, and till lately the gallows were standing: such frightful exhibitions, we trust, will not long disgrace a country which, by its belief in the *Christian* Scriptures repudiates the right of man to slay his fellow, from whatever cause.

About a mile east of Maidstone, is *The Mote*, Lord Romney's seat— the ancient possession of the Leybournes, and afterwards of the well-known but ill-fated Woodvilles (one of whom was father to Elizabeth, the consort of Edward IV.), after whom it came successively, either by descent or delineation, to the Wyatts, the Tuftons, and the Marshams, of the last of whom the present possessor is a direct descendant. The park comprises some 600 acres, and is well timbered with fine beeches and superb old oaks, and in front of the mansion is a broad canal, crossed by a bridge. The mansion itself stands on an eminence, commanding a large portion of the park and neighbourhood; it is quite a modern and somewhat plain edifice, built of stone, but very handsome in the interior, and having many splendid family and other pictures well worthy of a visit. The late earl was a most munificent benefactor to the whole district in which he lived; and his successor still patronises the leading institutions of the town, in which, as the chief landholder and lord of the manor, he exercises a most powerful interest.

*Malling Abbey*, too, and *Allington Castle* deserve a passing notice ere finally leaving Maidstone. The former of these, close by the village of the same name, to the north of the town, is approached by a fine old gateway, much of which is still intact. A handsome old tower, an oratory, and extensive walls, foundations, &c., indicate the prior existence of a most extensive monastery. As for *Allington Castle*, the property of the Wyatts, which stands on the left bank of the Medway, about a mile below the town, it possesses no inconsiderable historical interest; for, independently of prior family claims to distinction, Sir Henry Wyatt was made a banneret and Knight of the Bath, as well as reinstated in his forfeited possessions, as the reward of his attachment to the cause of Henry VII. He and his son both successively entertained here the burly, licentious Henry VIII., whose jealousy, however, was excited by the admiration which his accomplishments elicited from the hapless Anne Boleyn, the murdered wife of that ruthless sovereign. It afterwards belonged to the Astley family, and from them—like the manor of Maidstone—descended to the Earls of Romney. The grounds have long been disparked, and the castle has been suffered to fall into decay; but it still has extensive remains, including an arched gateway and interior court-yard surrounded by ancient buildings. It is now used as a farm-house.

*Leybourne, Bradbourne, Aylesford*, and several other places, all more or less interesting to the antiquarian and the lover of nature, might here claim to be described: but as this is a railway guide—that is, a companion for railway travellers to indicate their whereabout from one place to another, and tell them of the principal objects of interest on the road, and not much out of it—we must avoid all temptations to discursiveness, and quietly return to the Paddock-Wood Station, where, no doubt, the Folkestone and Dover carriage folks have been awaiting us with no little impatience.

# CHAPTER V.

Brenchley—Staplehurst—Cranbrook and Sissinghurst Castle—Bethersden and the Lovelaces—Tenterden and its Steeple—Godington and East Sutton—Leeds Castle—Eastwell Park and the Earl of Winchelsea—Ashford Town, Station, and Workshops.

Resuming our journey on the main line from the Paddock-Wood Station, and passing through a country which owes much of its beauty to the pleasing undulations of its surface, we see on the south the ancient village of *Brenchley*, remarkable for the large, antique-looking houses that it contains, as well as for a clump of trees near it, called Brenchley Toll, which from its elevation is a striking object, visible for many miles in every direction; and not far from it is *Horsmonden*, a village of very similar appearance to the preceding, the neighbourhood of which abounds with noble old oaks of enormous size and great value.

The fifty-first mile from the London Terminus brings the traveller to Marden, an intermediate station—four miles to the south of which is *Boughton Monchelsea*, which derives the latter name from the Monchensies or Monchelseas, who formerly possessed the land here; but it is more commonly called *Boughton Quarry*, owing to the large quantity of Kentish rag-stone quarried on the hills to the south of the village. On the hill-side stands the church, an interesting old structure; and almost adjoining the churchyard is the fine estate of Boughton Place, the house of which, situated in a spacious, well-wooded park, commands an extensive view over the Weald of Kent.

Two short miles further, and we arrive at Staplehurst Station, near a pretty village of that name, the church and old timber-built houses of which are well worth attention from the artist as well as the antiquary. At this point, also, the lover of ancient architecture may, by a walk of about five miles, indulge himself with a view of Cranbrook and Sissinghurst Castle: the former a pleasant little town agreeably situated near the centre of the Weald, and remarkable for its very fine and spacious old church, one of the handsomest in the country—the latter an interesting ruin of a noble seat that once belonged to the Saxenhursts and Bakers, but of which the great entrance and some out-offices are all that now remain, though less than a hundred years ago the buildings were entire.  The foundations are very extensive, and the representations of it by Hasted, in his " History of Kent," indicate a mansion of great extent; the place is well worthy of a visit, and the artist will find about it an abundance of subjects for the exercise of his pencil.  At no great distance, also, is *Finchcocks*, originally belonging to a family of that name, but which afterwards descended to the Bathursts, one of whom erected the present noble mansion, which is beautifully situated in a spacious, well-timbered park.

Fifty-six miles from London is the HEADCORN STATION, another intermediate station; at no great distance from which is *Chart Sutton*, near which is the fine seat and park of the Des Bouveries, the house most beautifully situated, overlooking the Weald and its contiguous districts.  The neighbourhood, also, is said to have been formerly planted in vineyards, from the produce of which considerable quantities of excellently-flavoured wine were made.  *Sutton Valence*, too, though now an insignificant village, deserves notice as having been the property of the Valences, formerly a powerful baronial family in this district; and near it are the venerable ivy-mantled ruins of *Sutton Castle,* which, from the remains of the keep and walls, appears to have been strongly fortified, and may perhaps have been used as a place of defence for its lords during the wars of the barons.  The churches of both these villages are good specimens of the grave Norman style, and contain within them some good carvings and interesting monumental brasses.

The railway, after passing the villages of Smarsden and Bedenham, which both lie on the south side, reaches the PLUCKLEY STATION at the sixty-second mile from London; not far from which, still on the south side, is *Bethersden*, the ancient seat of the Lovelaces (a family of no small military renown in the fourteenth and fifteenth centuries), but of which there are now no remains, the place being principally celebrated for its quarries of marble, of the same character as that found at Petworth, in Sussex—a very hard and durable building-material, susceptible of a good polish, and much used in the embellishment of Canterbury and Rochester Cathedrals, as well as of many ancient mansions in this part of Kent.  The next parish to Bethersden is that of *Great Chart*, the village of which, with the church, occupies the summit of a ridge of hills, and near it may be seen the ruins of a market-place, indicating it to have been once of much larger size and importance than at present.  It may be mentioned, also, that nine miles south of the

Pluckley Station is the small market-town of *Tenterden*, very prettily situated on an eminence that commands a great extent of country southward, and having a noble church, the tower and steeple of which are used as a landmark by mariners coming up the British Channel. The old story of Tenterden steeple having been the cause of the Goodwin Sands, is, according to Fuller, derived from the fact that an abbot of St. Augustine's, Canterbury, who was also rector of this parish, misapplied certain funds set aside for the purpose of keeping the sea-walls of certain lands, previously the property of Goodwin, Earl of Kent, to the erection of this steeple, in consequence of which the sea broke over and submerged them, converting them into what are now called the *Goodwin Sands.* This, it must be confessed, is rather a lame account; but we must be content to accept it in the absence of a better. On the north side of the line, within a moderate distance of Pluckley, are several extensive estates which require notice. First of all we have *Godington*, the noble residence of the house of Toke, who boast of a lineal descent from the Sire de Touque, who came over with William the Conqueror, and fought at the battle of Hastings—a building partly ancient, partly modernised, and well worth inspection, on account of its oak-carvings, stained-glass windows, and family portraits: it stands in a fine park of about 600 acres, planted by a celebrated landscape-gardener of the last century. The church, also, is a handsome Norman structure with a lofty steeple at its west end; and in the interior are some fine old monuments of the Tokes. Then comes *East Sutton*, once a part of the possessions of Odo, the Conqueror's half-brother, and which, after passing successively into the hands of Aylmer, Earl of Pembroke, Lord Grey de Ruthyn, and others, came at last, in 1610, by purchase, to Sir Edward Filmer, to whose descendants it still belongs. The present house is mostly modern, and stands in a park tastefully laid out and thickly clothed with forest trees, chiefly oaks and ashes, and fronting the mansion is a fine piece of water. The church stands near the summit of a hill overlooking the park. *Ulcombe*, the ancient seat of the St. Ledgers—now of the Clerkes; *Boughton Malherbe*, the property of the Woottons from the time of Richard II., and the birthplace of the accomplished Sir Henry Wootton, who had the confidence successively of Queen Elizabeth and James I.; *Chelston*, the property of J. S. Douglas, Esq.; and *Harrietsham Place*, all in this neighbourhood, are well worthy of a passing visit. But we have now to direct our fellow-traveller's attention to one of those fine baronial castles of which Kent once boasted so many glorious examples.

*Leeds Castle* is supposed to have been built by the Crevecœurs, from whom it passed to Lord Badlesmere, who was hung for rebellion in the reign of Edward II. In the fourteenth century it was inhabited by William of Wykeham, and early in the following by Archbishop Arundel, on whose death it reverted to the Crown: it was conveyed early in the sixteenth century to Antony St. Ledger, whose son alienated the estate to Sir Richard Smith, the heiresses of whom sold it to Sir Thomas Colpepper, and thence it descended, by marriage, to Lord Fairfax, whose nephew and heir, Dr. Denny, was the ancestor of the present proprietor, Wickham Martin, Esq. The castle is an imposing but irregular stone pile, of many dates and styles of architecture, encircled by a deep moat, which is supplied by a tributary stream of the Medway, and standing in a beautiful park, supplied with an abundance of old, umbrageous timber trees. The approach to the mansion is over a bridge of two arches and through a gateway, which, from its style of architecture, was a part probably of the original castle built by the Crevecœurs; and beyond is a handsome court, round which is formed that part which contains the chief apartments. The front is uniform and built of stone, the windows are arched in the Gothic style, and the whole is surmounted by an embattled parapet. At the rear of the castle, likewise, united to it by an ancient bridge, is a large building, of considerable beauty, which was probably used as the castle-keep. Besides those portions still kept in repair, there are some interesting ruins, supposed to have formed a part of the fortifications and out-offices. Indeed, this castle is, on the whole, one of the finest extant specimens of Norman architecture in this country, and will amply repay even an extended examination.

*Charing*, a village about five miles and a half north-east of Pluckley Station, is celebrated as having been once the site of a palace belonging to the see of Canterbury; and near the church may be seen very extensive remains, including a gateway, chapel, and refectory. The whole of this estate was given up at the Reformation, and sold. At the distance of about two miles hence we come to another noble seat— *Eastwell Park*—the property of the ancient family of the Finches, whose present representative is the tenth Earl of Winchelsea. The park comprises about 2000 acres of some of the finest land in Kent, having a very varied surface of hill and dale, and commanding in its more elevated parts a prospect, both north and south, many miles in extent, from Sheerness on one side, to the Channel and France on the other: it is tastefully laid out, and contains some noble forest trees; besides which it is abundantly stocked with deer. The mansion, which stands at the north-east corner of the park, is a modern structure, built by Bonomi on a very magnificent scale, with a most imposing frontage, and containing in its interior a suite of splendid state apartments, most gorgeously furnished, with accommodation for a very large number of guests, besides most extensive offices, stabling, &c., and some tastefully arranged gardens. The visitor of the park must not forget to see Eastwell Church, which, besides several monuments of the Finches, contains in its chancel a curious old tomb of one Richard Plantagenet, whom tradition reports to have been the son of Richard III. As an ecclesiastical structure, however, it is incomparably surpassed by that in the neighbouring parish of *Boughton-Aluph*, a cross-church of great beauty, and, though much dilapidated, showing the traces of no little former splendour. To the north of Pluckley, also, are two other estates of considerable importance— *Hothfield Place*, the seat of the Earl of Thanet; and *Surrenden-Dering*, the property of Sir Edward C. Dering, Bart., in whose family it has been vested more than four centuries, both of them handsome mansions, well situated so as to command extensive views of the surroundg country, and surrounded by well-wooded parks.

ASHFORD TOWN AND STATION, FROM THE LINE.

Four miles beyond Pluckley and sixty-seven from London, is the
ASHFORD STATION, a principal and very important station, not only as
being the junction-point of the Canterbury and Isle of Thanet branch,
as well as of a minor branch to Rye and Hastings, but also as being
the chief depôt and carriage-factory of the South-Eastern Railway
Company.  The town itself is nearly a mile from the station, and is
chiefly modern, consisting of a wide street, in the centre of which is
the market-house, while the church, a large and well-proportioned
structure, stands at its east end; besides which, adjacent to the station,
is a hamlet of quite recent construction, inhabited by the railway
workmen and their families, for whose use a new church has recently
been erected, with an adjoining school-house.  A mechanic's institution was established in 1846, and two years later a handsome brick
building was erected for the London and County Bank.  With a few
words concerning the charities of the town, we are, for want of space,
compelled to close this brief sketch.  In the year 1574 three-and-a-
half acres of ground at Burrow Hill was given in trust by one Richard
Best, who directed the profits of the land to be employed for the poor.
This charity now produces 12l. 7s. 6d. per annum.  In the year 1625
Thomas Milles bequeathed for the poor of Ashford 200l., to be employed for stock, &c., to set them to work.  This sum, with 50l. given
by Richard Smith, was also expended in the purchase of land.  John
Barlow, by will, bequeathed in the year 1520, 100l., the interest to
be laid out yearly in bread.  The station is a double one, very
nearly resembling those at the Reigate and Maidstone junctions.
The depôt comprises a large engine-shed, 208 feet long and 64 feet
broad (over which is a tank holding 55,000 gallons of water), a car-

ASHFORD ENGINE WORKS, &c.

riage and truck house 645 feet in extent, capable of containing fifty
carriages and eighty trucks, with a general store-room 216 feet long
and 40 feet wide. The workshops extend to a length of 396 feet, with
an uniform breadth of 45 feet, being divided into two compartments,
one for repairing engines and provided with a powerful traversing
crane; the other, the machine-shop or turnery, where the finishing of
the engine-work is done. There is, also, a smith's shop, with twenty
forges, which is altogether 175 feet long and 45 feet broad; a boiler
and wheel-hooping shop, of nearly similar dimensions; and a tender
shop of about half the size of the above. All these departments are
conducted, under a resident engineer, by a staff of nearly 500 workmen.

## CHAPTER VI.

Mersham Hatch, the Seat of the Knatchbulls—Mountmorris and Beechborough
Park—Westenhanger and its Ruins—Saltwood Tunnel and Castle—Folkestone
Town and Harbour—Shakspeare's Cliff and its Tunnel—Dover Town, Harbour,
Castle, &c.—Environs of Dover.

PROCEEDING onwards towards Dover, the first object requiring notice
is *Mersham Hatch*, which has been the property of the Knatchbulls
since the reign of Henry VII. The present mansion, which stands on
Mersham Heath, facing the south, is a modern stone erection, built
during the last and present century, and consisting of a centre and two
wings, tastefully embellished with quoins, balustrades, and other ornaments, having its interior of a grandeur fully corresponding with its
exterior beauty. The park is very extensive and well wooded, with a
handsome sheet of water in its lower part. The present possessor is
Sir Edward Knatchbull, Bart., who has long ranked as one of the most
influential landed proprietors in the county. The fifteen miles of railway between Ashford and Folkestone cross for the most part the
southern edge of the chalk-downs that run eastward to Dover, and contain fewer objects of interest than the country previously traversed.
The antiquary, however, will find himself repaid by a visit to *Liminge
Church*, situated on an eminence to the north of the line, and to a
Roman barrow below it; for this village is supposed to be on one of
the ancient Roman roads leading from Lenham, through Saltwood, to

Dover. *Monks-Horton Priory*, also, a work of the twelfth century, is a fine ruin, presenting some good and very perfect specimens of Norman mouldings and sculptures. Further on we pass *Mount Morris*, the seat of Lord Rokeby, a heavy brick structure, one of those so common to the early part of the last century, but standing in a fine, well-wooded park of nearly 1000 acres, about a third of which consists of excellent pasture-land; the heights at the back of the park command a most extensive view of the South-downs, the Channel, and the coast of France. At no great distance from the line, also in this direction, is *Beechborough Park*, anciently the property of the Valaigns, but which, since the reign of Elizabeth, has belonged to the Brockman family, the present representative of whom is William Brockman, a gentleman highly respected in this part of Kent. The house, which was almost rebuilt in the middle of the last century, stands in the midst of grounds most picturesquely laid out, though withal rather too formally for the present taste of landscape gardening. It may be observed here, also, that the line passes almost immediately to the north of the extensive level of Romney Marsh, which may occasionally be seen from the carriages.

At the completion of the seventy-fifth mile is the WESTENHANGER and HYTHE STATION, an intermediate station used principally by the inhabitants of the ancient port of Hythe and the graziers on Romney Marsh. The town of *Hythe* is of no great size, but respectably built, clean, and healthy, being also most picturesquely situated at the foot of a steep hill, and extending down close to the sea. It is occasionally frequented by visitors, for whom there are inns, lodging-houses, libraries, &c.; and on the hills above, which command extensive views, are some pretty villas. West of the town are some fine barracks for the staff-corps, with a good house for the commandant. The church stands on the hill-side at the top of the town, and has a light, elegant tower surmounted by four turrets. Hythe is one of the Cinque Ports, and, as such, enjoyed the privilege of sending two members to Parliament down to the Reform Act, which deprived it of one of its members. It formerly had a corporation, now decayed; and, but for the visitors in summer, it has few claims to notice, being chiefly inhabited by pilots and fishermen. Not far from it, close on the shore, is *Sandgate Castle*, built in the reign of Henry VIII., but much altered, as well as thoroughly repaired, at the commencement of the present century, in order that it might serve as a defence against the French; it mounts ten 24-pounders, is bomb-proof throughout, and has accommodation for forty artillerymen. Near the fort is a scattered fishing village, and on the heights around are some pretty-looking houses, mostly occupied by visitors during summer.

We must now conduct the traveller to the ruins of *Westenhanger*, which lie almost in the same direction, and within sight of Hythe. The demesne originally belonged to the Aubervilles, and thence passed by marriage to Nicholas de Criol, of Ostenhanger, from whom it descended, with other estates, to Sir Edward Poyning, who commenced here a magnificent mansion, afterwards completed by Henry VIII., who also greatly enlarged the park and estate. Queen Elizabeth once stayed here some days during one of her progresses; and she afterwards, no doubt for an ample consideration, granted the castle and manor to Thomas Smythe (ancestor of Viscount Strangford), who farmed the Customs of the port of London. The " Customer," as he was called, greatly added to the beauty of the mansion, and improved the grounds. The estate afterwards came to the Finch family, who pulled down a large part of the edifice for the sake of the materials, and afterwards sold the estate to the Champneis family, whose descendants still possess it. The present ruins, small as they are, indicate Westenhanger to have been a most extensive and noble pile of building. Its site was moated all round, and it had a drawbridge, large gatehouse, and portcullis, being surrounded, also, by very high and enormously thick walls, embattled throughout, fortified by nine great towers, and having a gallery communicating from tower to tower. One of them, indeed, is called *Fair Rosamond's*, from a tradition that this unhappy favourite of Henry II. was confined here; but this seems very doubtful. Hasted, also, from whom our description is chiefly taken, makes mention of a long upper room, called her gallery, in which she was imprisoned; but, after all, the evidence of her having been here is very slight, depending chiefly on the discovery of a sceptred hand, supposed to have been part of a statue of Henry II. On how small a peg do antiquarians sometimes hang their pretty stories! The parts now remaining are the walls and two towers on the north and east sides, the chapel, and a portion of the great entrance, with a portion of the garden walls; but portions of the garden walls are constantly crumbling and falling into the moat, while the remainder is covered with ivy, or overgrown with trees—the whole a lamentable monument of the Vandalic contempt with which its modern owners regarded the noble piles of antiquity.

The line, after passing the Westenhanger Station, runs to the east of Barham Downs, a place of some celebrity in ancient times, and still exhibiting the remains of Roman encampments, with vast numbers of tumuli, &c., in which coins, urns, and other articles, clearly Roman, have been discovered. These downs, also, were at different times the cenes of large armed assemblages—as in the time of King John, who assembled here an army of 60,000 men to repel a threatened invasion of the French under Philip le Bel, and in those of the barons, who met here under Simon de Montfort in the reign of Henry III., not to mention frequent encampments here during the last long war with France. Close to these downs, also, is *Barham Court*, which for many years belonged to the Fitzwises, who afterwards called themselves Barhams, but which has been vested for the last two centuries in the family of the Deerings, of whom C. Deering, Esq., is the present representative. Near the seventy-ninth mile the railway enters *Saltwood Tunnel*, 952 yards long, cut through chalk and gravel; and not far from this part of the line are two objects of considerable interest— *Sandling Park*, the beautiful demesne of W. Deedes, Esq., and the venerable ruin of *Saltwood Castle*, which will amply repay the antiquary's attention. The latter, which was most probably erected in the reign of Henry I., or possibly even earlier, by Hugo de Mountford, the possessor of the manor at the time of the Conquest, stands on a commanding elevation, and occupies with its enclosing walls a nearly elliptical area of about four acres. Its entrance is by a gateway, now in ruins, defended by a portcullis and flanked by two lofty towers; the whole building being surrounded by a broad and deep moat. The court of the old castle is now filled with barns formed out of the ruins; but at its further end are the remains of the entrance-hall, which goes through to the back, and led originally into an inner court, though it is now divided into two apartments. In these apartments, one of which is vaulted and groined, the principal ornament is the Tudor rose, which was added most probably by Archbishop Courtenay, who made large additions to the mansion (as may be seen from his arms impaled with those of the see of Canterbury), and annexed to it a spacious park. The round towers contain hexagonal chambers, some of which, as well as others in the building, are still inhabited by farm servants. The walls of the inner court are polygonal, approaching the form of a circle ; and on its south side are the ruins of the chapel (which is early English), and of some other buildings, the destination of which is now unknown. The hall, the great banqueting-room, and some other fine apartments, with minor offices, still remain ; and, at any rate, there is quite enough even now visible to warrant the conviction that this must at one time have ranked among the noblest of our baronial halls. It need scarcely be added that the roof of the castle commands a most extended view of the scenery seaward, terminated in the horizon by the white cliffs about Boulogne. A paved way, it may be added, is still to be seen on the hill leading from Hythe to the castle ; and hence it has been conjectured that a fortress stood here even as early as the time of the Romans. At no great distance from the castle is the church : nd thisappears to have been built about the time of Edward III.— it contains several good specimens of Norman arches, and the east exhibits traces of painted glass. In the chancel, too, is an oaken window chest of very curious and elaborate workmanship, well worthy of examination.

EXHIBITION ENGINE.

FOLKESTONE JUNCTION.

FOLKESTONE HARBOUR AND HARBOUR STATION, INCLINE. AND COMPANY'S VESSELS (STARTING-PLACE FOR BOULOGNE).

A very short ride now takes us into the FOLKESTONE JUNCTION STATION, where the carriages going on to Dover are separated from those proceeding to Folkestone; and another short mile brings us at the eighty-second mile from London to one of the leading termini of the line, FOLKESTONE, which has been vastly improved, both as respects size and prosperity, since the South-Eastern Railway Company have taken such pains to improve the port, with the view of making it a packet station to compete with Dover. The town is very irregularly built in its lower and older part, having steep and narrow streets, which nevertheless are clean and well paved, and the whole is now lighted with gas. The higher portion, however, going up to the cliffs, is much more regular, and comprises several pretty terraces with lodging-houses for summer visitors, who may here enjoy all the benefits of a fine, bracing air, and sea-bathing, combined with that rural retirement so desirable in the country, and which cannot be found either at Dover, Ramsgate, or other bathing towns on this coast. The cliffs, too, command the most delightful views, south-west, over the wide level of Romney Marsh, as far as Beachy Head, while seaward stands the town and harbour at our feet, beyond which are the Straits of Dover, skirted in the horizon by the coast of France. Folkestone has two churches— one of modern erection in the upper town—and four or five places of worship for Dissenters, all of which have attached Sunday-schools; besides which there are several daily subscription-schools, besides a good grammar-school. It has also a town-hall and market-house, a custom-house, a mechanics' institute, dispensary, several libraries, reading-rooms, &c., and four or five good inns. As respects the last, however, none can compete with the *Pavilion*—a most magnificent hotel, built a few years since by the railway company, and which far exceeds in size, splendour, and convenience most of the hotels in our large towns, furnishing the traveller, too, with every luxury he can desire at prices much lower than at most English hotels. Recently, it has been enlarged, under the proprietorship of Mr. Breach, by the addition of a *table d'hôte* saloon, coffee-room, billiard-rooms, &c., the whole now furnishing accommodation for several hundred guests, besides private resident families.

The port of Folkestone, not less than the town, has been vastly improved by the South-Eastern Company. Even before they acquired

VIEW IN FOLKESTONE.

possession of it in 1845, some efforts had been made by the construction
of an arm at the end of the pier to arrest the progress of shingle, which
here, as at Dover, constantly choked and filled up the harbour; but they
were insufficient, and the evil, indeed, was increased thereby rather
than diminished, for at neap tides it could not be entered by vessels
drawing more than nine or ten feet of water, and it was no unusual
thing for a vessel to be neaped for days at the very entrance; thus not
only uselessly detaining itself, but blocking up the channel so as to prevent the entrance of all other craft.  The first step adopted by the company for arresting the shingle was the carrying out from the south-
west end of the arm of the pier of a groyne formed with piles, and
which gradually led to the formation of a breakwater, about fifty feet
broad at top, forming an obtuse angle with the old arm of the pier.
This at once stopped the further accumulation of shingle within the
harbour, which was then at vast expense cleared of the gravel and mud
long collected therein, and it has since remained clear.  This breakwater, moreover, has been greatly improved by constructions of masonry
intended to bind the work together; and at the same time great additions and improvements have been made both in the foundations and
superstructures of the original piers.  In fact, Folkestone Harbour

which was before a slough of gravel and mud, almost inaccessible except at half-spring or spring tides, has, owing to these improvements, become " a harbour having twenty feet of water considerably within the entrance, and is now capable of being entered by steamers three hours and a half after high water; while during neap tides there are occasionally four or five feet of water in the entrance at low water, and immediately outside, sufficient for a steamer to take her passengers from the pier-head and work herself clearly off." (See *Mr. Swan's Report.*) Another point of importance in connexion with this harbour, is the great ease with which it can be taken in bad weather, to which the captains of steamers bear almost individual testimony; and to this, also, we may add the superior ease with which vessels may be swung, and the facility of backing out without turning round, so as to save time in landing passengers and again leaving port. On On the whole, this harbour, as now improved, is one of the finest monuments of engineering skill in this country, and confers infinite honour on Peter W. Barlow, Esq., the company's engineer, and the Directors, who so spiritedly backed the undertaking. It scarcely need be added that the first result of these improvements was to make Folkestone suited for a regular packet station, and now for some years this port has acquired at least one-half of the traffic across the Straits, which was formerly wholly monopolised by the neighbouring port of Dover; now, as the sea voyage is shorter, and the steamers are vastly superior, can there be any doubt that ere long it will become the chosen route of all the intelligent travelling public? Indeed, the constantly and rapidly increasing customs and harbour dues of the port, year by year, furnish of themselves a sufficient proof that Folkestone has acquired a vigour and vitality which it only requires perseverance in the inhabitants to maintain; nor can this increase in the prosperity of the town be truly ascribed to any other cause than the spirited conduct of the company, who have made it one of their most important maritime termini. The census, moreover, speaks on this subject with an eloquence that is quite unanswerable, for in 1831 Folkestone had only 2300 inhabitants, and in 1841 but 2900, whereas in 1851 it had upwards of 7500; showing an increase of about 140 per cent. Facts like these speak more than all praise!

We are reluctant to leave Folkestone without a word in favour of a really good seminary—Grove House—conducted by Mr. Clark. Here the moral and religious training of the pupil forms a positive part of the education instilled.   In these days this is surely an important consideration for parents.

Hie we on now to Dover—a place of world-wide celebrity, six miles beyond Folkestone.  The line between these points presents features of the greatest possible interest, not only on account of the fine marine views which it furnishes, but also by reason of the extraordinary engineering difficulties that were to be overcome in its construction.   Immediately out of Folkestone the railway passes over a viaduct of nineteen uniform arches, thirty feet each in span, crossing the small river Foord ; the greatest height from the river below being 100 feet, and its total length 780 feet.

FOLKESTONE VIADUCT.

From this point onwards the line is carried alternately through chalk cliffs, and on artificial embankments of the same material, and of such strength as to have successfully withstood the storms of the Channel ever since their construction.   The tunnels are three in number. First, the *Martello-tunnel*, about a mile and a half from the Folkestone junction, which is 636 yards in length ; secondly, the *Abbott's-cliff-tunnel*, the longest on the line, being 1940 yards from end to end ; and

VIEW FROM JUNCTION (OR OLD) STATION, FOLKESTONE.

thirdly, the *Shakspeare-cliff-tunnel*, 1393 yards long, so called, because
it runs through the celebrated Shakspeare-cliff,

> Whose high and bending head
> Looks fearfully on the confined deep,

and which has been so sublimely described by our immortal poet in his
tragedy of " King Lear." To realise the bard's description, however, the
tourist must ascend to its summit, 576 feet high; and then, if he has
nerve to withstand the grandeur of the scene below, he will see the
truth of *the following grand description:*

> How fearful
> And dizzy 'tis to cast one's eyes so low.
> The crows and choughs that wing the midway air
> Show scarce so gross as beetles; halfway down
> Hangs one that gathers samphires—dreadful trade!
> Methinks he seems no bigger than his head.
> The fishermen that walk upon the beach
> Appear like mice; and yon tall bark,
> Diminish'd to her cock—her cock a buoy
> Almost too small for sight: the murmuring surge
> That on the unnumber'd idle pebbles chafes
> Cannot be heard so high.   I'll look no more,
> Lest my brain turns, and the deficient sight
> Topple down headlong.

To return to the tunnel excavated in this world-known cliff, it consists of two separate tubes, each thirty feet high, and of Saracenic architecture, faced throughout with brickwork, except in such places where the hardness of the chalk rendered such precautions unnecessary, the whole being ventilated by seven shafts, sunk perpendicularly from the surface above, and the same number of lateral outlets towards the face of the cliff, originally made for the purpose of throwing the excavated matter into the sea below. The sea-wall leading to it from the Folkestone side is, likewise, well worthy of minute observation, as being one of the largest works of this nature in the kingdom; it is nearly three-quarters of a mile long, and elevated from sixty to seventy feet above the beach, being composed entirely of flint and shingles, consolidated into a compact mass with lime, thrown down to form the slantings of the cliff. A great quantity of this chalk, it may be observed, was obtained from the blasting of Roundown-cliff, which was effected with consummate skill by the use of 19,000 lbs. of gunpowder, causing the disintegration of no less than 400,000 cubic yards of rock, which in ten seconds, without noise or accident, were distributed over eighteen acres, causing a saving to the Railway Company of about 7000*l.* The viaduct on the Dover side, though of a different and less stupendous character, is no less interesting as a result of engineering science; it is about half a mile long, and formed of heavy beams of timber securely framed and bolted together, but left open so as to offer less resistance to the waves in stormy weather and spring-tides. The station at the Dover terminus is a double one, like those at Reigate, Tunbridge, and other leading stations; besides which, it is provided with ample accommodation for goods and waiting-rooms for passengers, while awaiting the trains or the examination of their luggage by the Custom-house officers, when arriving by the packets from the Continent. All the arrangements, too, are admirably made here, as well as at Folkestone, for shortening the delays to which travellers are usually subjected in leaving or arriving at our outports; and on this score the greatest credit is due to the South-Eastern Company, who first brought them into operation.

Dover (or as it is vulgarly called *Dovor*) is, as all the world knows, a great seaport and *point de départ* for foreigners leaving England for France and Belgium; besides which, it is the principal of the Cinque

RAILWAY AND TUNNEL UNDER SHAKSPEARE'S CLIFF, DOVER.

Ports, and as such received vast improvements under the energetic superintendence of the late Lord Warden—our lamented Iron Duke. It is situated in a deep valley of depression in the chalk ridges that form this line of coast, which depression also runs a considerable distance inward, forming the bed of the river Dour, which empties itself into the harbour. The old town consists of one principal thoroughfare, called Snargate-street, which extends upwards of a mile in a semicircular direction, following that of the valley on which it is built— shorter streets branching from it in both directions, together with ranges of modern-built houses along the shore. The older part is very irregularly built, narrow, and ill-kept; but vast improvements have been made within the last few years—several new streets and terraces, lined with well-appointed shops and splendid mansions, have been erected; and the private residences for the summer visitors on the Marine Parade, Waterloo Crescent, Esplanade, &c., form, with other streets, a continuous range of imposing buildings, that extends from the north-pier to the foot of the Castle-cliff. Several of the older streets have likewise been considerably widened; and Dover has, on the whole, made wonderful progress during the last ten or fifteen years. The buildings also have extended so much inwards along the valley of the Dour, that the villages of Charlton and Buckland have become continuous parts of the town.

Dover boasted in former times of a large number of churches and conventual establishments; but most of these have long disappeared. The oldest extant churches are St. James's and St. Mary's: the former being an Anglo-Saxon structure, the latter early Norman, recently restored in excellent taste at an expense of nearly 6000*l.* St. Mary's deserves notice, also, as containing the tomb of Foote, the English Aristophanes. Trinity Church is a modern erection in the ornamental English style, and was built at a cost of 8000*l.* In the adjacent hamlets, also, of Charlton, Buckland, and Hougham, there are four churches, nearly all either rebuilt or modern. The only conventual building now remaining is St. Martin's Priory, in the churchyard of which lie the remains of the poet Churchill, who died in 1764, and whose monument was restored by the late Lord Byron. The priory itself is now a mere ruin, and occupied as a farm-house; but the refectory and gateway are well worthy of a visit from the antiquarian; and the old church of the Maison Dieu, now turned into a town-hall and gaol, merits similar attention. Dover has likewise ten places of worship for Dissenters, including a Roman Catholic chapel and Jews' synagogue, with chapels for Independents, Baptists, Wesleyan Methodists, and Unitarians; to all of which, as well as the churches, large Sunday-schools are attached, furnishing religious instruction to upwards of 5000 children. There is also a large foundation-school, conducted on the national principle, and another at Charlton; besides which, there are Lancastrian schools, schools of industry, and infant schools, which furnish on the whole ample means of instruction for the poorer classes. Dover possesses, also, a military hospital, a dispensary, savings bank, and several minor charities. The principal public buildings are the town-hall and gaol, already mentioned; the theatre and post-office in Snargate-street, the market-house (above which is the Museum), the Assembly-rooms, and the Custom-house near the harbour.

The harbour, which may be said to be almost literally enclosed by the town, is worthy of the ancient reputation of the port, the entrance to it being now easily accessible during rough weather. It has no longer a bar of shingles at its entrance, which was a constant cause of accumulations inside. Great improvements have been made within the last few years, especially during the wardenship of the late Duke of Wellington. The harbour consists, in its present state, of an outer and inner basin, the former containing an area of $7\frac{1}{2}$ acres, the latter of $6\frac{1}{4}$ acres, both being kept clear by a *pent*, or backwater, of $11\frac{1}{2}$ acres, with an entrance 60 feet wide. On the west side of the outer harbour is a wet dock, with an adjoining graving dock; the entrance between the pier-heads, which opens towards the S.S.E., being 110 feet wide, formed of stone and brickwork, faced with wooden piles: the depth at high water varies from 14 to 18 feet, therefore the harbour is dry at low water. It is still the station of the packet establishments for Calais and Ostend; and the Government has seven post-office packets under the superintendence of a commander in the navy. Packets, also, of private companies, run to Calais, Ostend, and London; and a small squadron is attached to this port belonging to the French Government. Dover, moreover, is the grand pilot-station of the Cinque Ports, having attached to it fifty-six pilots employed in the Channel-service, under the Lord Warden and Commissioners of the harbour. The port has only

DOVER HARBOUR AND HEIGHTS.

about 100 vessels of its own, all of small tonnage, employed chiefly as coasters; but it is visited annually by about 3000 sailing vessels and several hundred steamers, so that from one cause or another the harbour is generally well filled with shipping, and can be entered by vessels of more than 500 tons.

Dover has a thriving, busy trade, chiefly derived from the influx of passengers to and from the Continent, and its popularity as a place of fashionable resort for sea-bathing; besides which, it has large ship-building yards, sail and rope manufactories, paper and corn mills, &c., &c.; indeed, the place has altogether a bustling and prosperous appearance. The markets are held on Wednesdays and Saturdays; besides which, there are daily markets for provisions. A large annual fair used to be held in November; but the town has lately surrendered the charter. There are also two banking companies, being branches of the London and County and National and Provincial Bank of England. The borough is municipally divided into three wards, and is governed by a mayor, five other aldermen, and eighteen councillors, having also a borough debt-court under a recorder. Petty sessions are held in the town-hall; and here also are held Courts of Admiralty and Chancery for the Cinque Ports. The constable of the castle, also, still possesses the jurisdiction of a sheriff within the Cinque Port limits—writs from the superior courts being directed to him, and his warrant executed by an officer called the Bodar; the debtors' prison, too, is within the castle, and under its constable's jurisdiction. Dover is, also, a parliamentary borough, and has returned two members to the House of Commons since the 18th Edward I.; its present members are Viscount Chelsea, the son of the Earl of Cadogan, and E. R. Rice, Esq.; the number of electors being about 2000.

Dover, however, owes its principal celebrity after all to its castle and fortifications on the heights surrounding the town. The former, which occupies a commanding eminence on the south-east side of the valley, is a most picturesque object, whether seen from sea or land, and comprises a vast mass of buildings of every age—British, Roman, Anglo-Saxon, Norman, and modern—occupying altogether an area of about thirty-two acres—the approach thereto being by a bold ascent leading to the castle-gates. The whole is well worthy of the antiquarian's notice, especially the remains of the old ramparts, a temple, bath, and pharos, which are certainly of Roman origin. The whole of its antiquities are well described in Mr. Rigden's excellent " Guide to Dover," to which the curious reader is referred, as the subject is too extensive for a book like the present. Some general notice, however, must be given of the castle, and particularly of its modern additions. Previously to the last French war the works had become greatly dilapidated; but they were then repaired and greatly enlarged. At present there are upper and lower courts, surrounded (except towards the sea) by curtains and large dry ditches; and in the centre of the upper court is a spacious keep, built by Henry III., now converted into a bomb-proof magazine; while the curtain of the lower court is flanked at irregular intervals by ten towers of various construction, the oldest built by Earl Godwin, the others at different times during the Norman dynasty; and these again communicate with the ditch by subterraneous passages. The modern works consist of batteries with heavy artillery, casemates, covered ways, barracks excavated in the chalk sufficiently large to accommodate 2000 men, magazines, a large cave, &c., with additional guard-houses and lines of defence. Neither must we omit to notice a fine piece of ordnance, commonly called " Queen Elizabeth's pocket-pistol," twenty-four feet long, presented to that sovereign by the States of Holstein, nor to mention a good collection of portraits of the successive lord wardens, which may be seen in the governor's house.

Strongly fortified, however, and highly elevated as is the castle itself, even its highest part is overlooked by the eminences (familiarly called " the heights") to the south-west and north-west, which were fortified at the close of the last century, and are now bristling in every direction with batteries and redoubts amply furnished with cannon, regular lines, curtains, counterscarps, fosses, excavated passages, and all other appliances of modern military art, the whole of which were constructed during the eleven years prior to the peace of 1814, at a vast expenditure, and giving employment to many thousands of soldiers, masons, and artificers. On these heights, too, directly above the town, are very capacious barracks for foot soldiers—the communication with which from below is by the military shaft, the entrance to which is in Snargate-street; and it consists of three spiral flights of 140 steps each, winding round a large shaft or tower, open at the top to admit light, and so contrived that a large body of men can descend simultaneously, so as to present a broad

front immediately on arriving at the bottom.  Above the barracks is
the Grand Redoubt; and to the south-west of the latter, still more
elevated, is the citadel, defended by numerous ditches, flanking and
masked batteries, &c.; besides which, the Government are now ac-
tively engaged in strengthening the fortifications by adding new works
of extraordinary magnitude, and increasing the supply of cannon,
 mmunition, &c.

SITE OF THE FALL IN JAN., 1853.

Our engraving exhibits the site of an extensive fall of cliff, which
took place in January of the present year, and which created great
sensation through the whole neighbourhood;—near which we may
notice, as one of the Antiquities of Dover, the *Ship Hotel*, erected in
1529, but partly rebuilt within the last few years.  It is now kept by
Mr. Birmingham, a most gentlemanly and obliging host, and is better
known than almost any in Europe, most of its crowned heads having at
one time or other sojourned there; and its appointments throughout
give unmistakeable indications of English comfort and excellent accommodation.

The history of Dover is too extensive a subject for a little work like the present; but it may not be altogether passed unnoticed. It was called *Dwffyrha*, or "a steep place," by the Britons, *Dubris* by the Romans, and *Dofra* by the Saxons. The Roman road, called Watling-street, ran hence direct to Canterbury, and traces of it are yet to be seen on Barham Downs; indeed, there can be no doubt that the Romans attached great importance to Dover as a military station. The town was anciently walled, and had ten gates, the remains of which were standing only a few years ago. In the earlier times of the Normans, also, both the town and castle were held in high esteem as places of strength and a principal key to the kingdom; and since that time, from reign to reign successively, Dover has maintained its position as the chief stronghold of our dominions.

The neighbourhood of Dover abounds with beautiful walks and drives; for, independently of the fine sea views that are commanded by the neighbouring cliffs, the roads along and near the valley of the **Dour** present numerous objects of interest to those who have leisure to examine them in detail. Beyond the suburb of Charlton is a deep space, called *King's Bottom*, which in olden times was the favourite resort of the knights belonging to the castle, for the purpose of tilting and other chivalric exercises; and from the remains of anchors and the planks of vessels, it would seem that the sea once penetrated up to this point. Again: after passing through Buckland, we reach the pretty village of *River*, beautifully situated in a country, whose surface rapidly alternates with lofty hills and deep valleys, the unenclosed downs rising abruptly northwards to a great height, while southward there is a deep slope, running close down to the Dour. The pretty neat cottages and church of this village have an extremely picturesque appearance from the Canterbury road; and at the same time, through the opening of the valley eastward, are seen the town of Dover, its stately castle, and across the Channel the lofty cliffs and hills near Boulogne. Not far from this village, also, are *Kearsney Abbey*, a pseudo-monastic modern mansion, built by the late Mr. Fector, and *Archer's Court*, the handsome seat of J. B. Sladen, Esq. At no great distance, likewise, is *Broome Hall*, the property of Sir Henry Oxenden—the mansion was built in the reign of Charles I., and the grounds about it have within the last few years been greatly improved. The village of *Ewell* deserves a visit,

DOVER.

Showing the Castle, Waterloo Crescent, Wellesley Terrace, Marine Parade, East Cliff, &c.

F

owing to the fact of its having formed a part of the possessions of the Knights Templars in the twelfth century ; but, though there is a building on an eminence north of the village, called *Temple Farm*, there are now no remains of their ancient mansion, which was destroyed by fire about a century ago. The site of their park, however, is still to be found a little distance off at Old Park Hill. At *Suringfield*, also, further to the south, was another establishment of the Knights Templars, of which there are some remains at a farm-house, including a chapel, two apartments, and extensive foundations. About three miles from Dover to the south of the Canterbury road are the interesting ruins of *St. Radigund's Abbey*, said to have been founded in 1191, and which was once of such importance, that its abbots were summoned to Parliament in the reign of Edward I. The walls cover a large extent of ground, and there are traces of a ditch and rampart. The gateway is in good preservation, and there are considerable remains of the chapel, as well as of the dwelling itself, which is now converted into a farm-house ; all the ruins are overgrown with ivy, which gives the whole a very picturesque appearance. On the high ground, again, about two miles north-west of River, is *Waldershare Park*, the principal seat of the Monins family, from whom it was purchased by Sir Henry Furnese, who erected the present noble mansion from the designs of Inigo Jones, and enclosed the park, planting it with long avenues of trees, according to the style of that period. The grounds, however, have subsequently been much extended, and are now extremely beautiful, commanding extensive views of all the surrounding country and the Channel beyond. The property now belongs to the Earl of Guildford, having descended to him by the marriage of a former earl with a sister of Sir Henry Furnese, the last male heir. While in this vicinity, moreover, the tourist must not forget to visit *Barfreston*, or *Baraton Church*, an undoubted specimen of Anglo-Saxon architecture, and which, though consisting only of a nave and chancel, and very small, yet contains within it a profusion of sculptures and grotesque ornaments, that indicate the great advances which art had made even at that early period. We have thus pointed out a few only of the objects of interest near Dover. The excursionist, who has leisure, will find many more for himself.

# CHAPTER VII.

## HASTINGS BRANCH.

Geological Features—Southborough—Tunbridge-Wells and its Environs—Eridge Castle and the Earl of Abergavenny—Bayham Abbey—Ticehurst and Roberts-bridge—Battle and its Abbey—St. Leonard's and its Architect—Hastings, Old and New, its Castle and Neighbourhood.

HAVING thus conducted the traveller along the main line to Dover and described at such length as our limits permit that celebrated fortress and stronghold, we shall now once more return to the junction station at Tunbridge, and take him by Tunbridge Wells and Battle to St. Leonard's and Hastings. Before we start, however, we must apprise our readers of a few geological features in this part of the line, which, at least for the first six miles, was through a series of cuttings and a tunnel of considerable length. The tunnel, in particular, offers some striking features, running through several remarkable strata, including beds of sandy brown clay passing into a dark blue clay divided by sandstone and ironstone, with traces of limestone containing fossils; and after passing the tunnel, alternating beds are seen of clay and sandstone, followed by a seam of white marl on a black clay closely resembling lignite. A little further, too, more black vegetable clay is visible, resting on sandstone quarried for buildings. The strata likewise change their character here, assuming a dome-like shape, and abruptly end in what is termed a *fault*, the sand-rocks having now disappeared and their places filled with clay. The whole distance, indeed, from Tunbridge to the Wells is full of geological interest on account of the depth and contortions of the strata, as well as the various colours of sand and clay, which are exposed by the cuttings.

The only place of interest between Tunbridge and the " Spa of Kent," is *Southborough*, the ancient possession of the Clare family, but which afterwards belonged to the Audleys and Staffords, from whom by the attainder of Stafford, Duke of Buckingham, for high treason in 1521, it fell to the Crown, and was afterwards purchased by *the customer* Smith of Westenhanger, in whose descendants it remained till the commencement of the present century. Southborough was the resort of the

TOAD-ROCK
TUNBRIDGE=WELLS STATION
ESPLANADE AT ST. LEONARD'S.

Court during the reign of the Merry Monarch, for the purpose of drinking the waters of the neighbouring spa; and the property commands most extensive views over this part of Kent.

Behold us now, after having passed through a dark tunnel, at the TUNBRIDGE WELLS STATION, curiously constructed in a sort of hollow, but admirably adapted in its various arrangements to accommodate the traffic of this favourite place of summer resort. We shall here pause for a while on our journey, in order to furnish our fellow-travellers with the general description of the " Spa" of Kent.

Tunbridge Wells, notwithstanding its present high repute, its large permanent population, amounting to upwards of 10,000 persons, is not a place of any standing as a fixed place of habitation, for although the healing properties of the waters were known as early as the beginning of the seventeenth century, and Queen Henrietta availed herself of these healing springs, as well as the queen and courtiers of the second Charles, yet even so recently as only sixty years ago it was the custom at the termination of each season to close not only the hotels and boarding-houses, but even the shops and houses generally till the approach of the following summer, the town being all but deserted during winter. It is situated forty-six miles from London and twenty-eight from Hastings by railway; and it lies in three parishes—Tunbridge, Speldhurst, and Frant—the latter of which is in Sussex. The Wells, indeed, is not a single place, but a district, comprising a series of scattered villages, mansions, and villas, within a circuit of three or four miles in diameter; and the principal parts are named from the surrounding eminences, as Mount Ephraim, Mount Sion, Mount Pleasant, and the Wells Proper; but by far the most beautiful quarter of this enchanting district lies to the north-east of the Wells Proper and beyond Mount Sion. It is called, from having been formerly a private estate, *Calverly Park;* nor can it be denied that the natural beauties derived from the variety of its surface and the richness of its verdure and foliage are much enhanced by the improvements of art and the erection of the pretty insulated villas that fringe its borders without destroying its park-like appearance. The original village forms what is now called the Wells Proper, where are the parade, the pump-room, and baths, two of the leading inns, the libraries, and the assembly-rooms, with the principal shops, many of which are on a scale of extent and splendour which may vie with those of Bath or Cheltenham. There is a modern market-house, and few places are better supplied with every kind of provisions, including fish, poultry, and fruit—the latter of very fine quality. The town has three churches—one old and little worthy of notice (having been built for the visitors, as a chapel of ease to Speldhurst)—two others, more modern, and tastefully built in the Gothic style, namely, Trinity Church, on Mount Pleasant, and Christ Church, on Mount Sion. The Roman Catholics have a handsome chapel, built of stone, in the Grosvenor-road; and there are four or five places of worship for different denominations of Dissenters. All the churches and chapels have their respective Sunday-schools; besides which, the Victoria national schools, a female British school, and an infant school, furnish ample means of instruction for the poorer classes of the inhabitants. There are also religious and medical charities; the poor, on the whole, being well cared for. A literary and scientific society is carried on with some spirit, and there is a horticultural society, the summer shows of which attract the beauty and fashion of the surrounding neighbourhood. A small theatre is generally open during the three summer months; but dramatic performances are but little encouraged. Races are annually held on the common, to the west of the town, in August; and in the neighbourhood are two packs of hounds.

Tunbridge Wells, till 1835, had no markets of its own, and was dependent on Tunbridge; but in that year a local act was passed, not only entitling it to the privileges of fairs and markets, but providing for the paving, lighting, police, &c., of the town, which is well supplied both with water and gas; few country towns, indeed, have a cleaner, neater, and more orderly appearance than the Wells. As respects trade, it has none beyond that maintained by the wants of the district and neighbourhood; nor is this by any means a cheap place of residence, as the prices of most articles, whether of constant consumption or otherwise, are by many degrees dearer than at Bath and other similar localities. The only branch, too, of native industry which may be termed a manufacture, is the formation of boxes, spoons, domino-boards, and a variety of articles in wood of various colours, formed in mosaic by a peculiar agglutinating process, familiarly known as Tunbridge-wares.

The precise period when the medicinal qualities of these mineral springs were discovered, cannot be ascertained; but they were, at any rate, greatly in vogue at the latter part of the seventeenth century. These springs, which occur in the beds of iron-sand, first rise north-west of the town in the obscure village of Speldhurst, and thence come down to the Wells, surging up at the lowest part of the narrow valley in which the original village was built. In 1664 Lord Muskerry surrounded the spring with a stone wall; but this has since been wholly covered in by means of a handsome stone building, containing cold, warm, shower, and vapour baths, adjoining to which is a spacious pump-room, opening on the parade. The water is a light, pure chalybeate, having a temperature of about 50° Fahr.; and its principal mineral ingredients are protoxide of iron, chloride of sodium, and sulphate of lime, in combination with carbonic acid gas. After all, however, the mineral constituents of these waters are very insignificant; for Sir Charles Scudamore, who accurately analysed them, discovered little more than a third of a grain of the protoxide of iron, about a sixth of a grain of common salt, and a little more than the fifth of a grain of sulphate of lime in a pint of water. However much, therefore, these waters may be valued for their virtues in cases of nervousness and dyspepsia, and however really beneficial they may be in female complaints, it is quite obvious that they have no claim to be compared for their active remedial qualities with those of Bath, Cheltenham, and Clifton. Its reputation stands, however, on quite independent grounds, for the beauty of the scenery in and around the Wells, the remarkable salubrity of the air, and the genteel, agreeable society of the place, will ever continue to give it popularity, and make it not only a favourite summer resort, but an eligible spot for permanent residence.

In every direction around the Wells are agreeable walks and rides, furnishing most extensive views of rural and forest scenery. Perhaps the most favourite ramble for pedestrians is across the common, on which are some curious rocks, known as the *Sweeps' Rocks;* and beyond is *Rusthall Common,* where may be seen another very extraordinary-looking object, called the *Toad Rock,* which somewhat resembles in shape the Lagganstones of Cornwall, and the form of which, it is evident, could only have been produced by natural causes. We have furnished so accurate a representation of it that it needs no further description. The *High Rocks,* likewise, about a mile and a half to the west of the Wells, are extremely well worth a visit: they range between forty and seventy feet in height, are composed of sandstone, and have several curious caverns near them which seem to have been rent asunder by some convulsion of nature. There are also several extremely delightful walks across the fields to the *Frant Forest, Twenty-acre Wood, Hall's Hole, Park Wood, &c.*

Resuming our places in the train, we shall now proceed southwards in the direction of Hastings—first, through a short tunnel directly after leaving the station, and then through a deep cutting to FRANT, where is a subordinate station three miles from the Wells. It is a pretty red-brick Elizabethan structure; and this, it may be observed, is the character of most of the stations on the Hastings branch, which is the most recent of the lines opened by the South-Eastern Company. To the west of Frant, but not visible from the line, stands the noble demesne of the Earl of Abergavenny, *Eridge Castle* (once one of the principal seats of the far-famed Neville family), an irregular, but splendid castellated Gothic pile, the front of which is almost covered with ivy and other creeping plants. It stands in a well-wooded and watered park, abundantly stocked with deer, and which comprises above 3000 acres of land, being also surrounded by about 10,000 more, all included within the estate. The park plantations have been arranged with consummate taste, and nurtured with such care, that many of the trees have attained an enormous growth; and within the park is a variety of rides (said to be altogether fifty-four miles in extent), which conduct to scenes of various characters, and occasionally embrace the most interesting objects in the adjacent country. The village of *Frant*, too, though not seen from the line, deserves notice: it is most romantically situated on the brow of a hill; and its handsome Gothic church, which stands on an eminence, commands, perhaps, one of the most extensive views in Kent, including the hills north-eastward to within a mile of Dover, the South-downs of Sussex, the hills about Sevenoaks, and those in the neighbourhood of Chatham, with Leith Hill and Box Hill in Surrey westward. The neighbourhood abounds with genteel villa-residences, among the prettiest of which is *Saxonbury Lodge*, a Gothic villa belonging to D. Rowland, Esq., the grounds of which are laid out with great taste, and command fine views of Eridge Park and the surrounding country. About three miles and a half, also, to the east of the line in this part of its course is *Bayham Abbey*, the demesne of the Marquis of Camden, originally built about the year 1200 for Premonstratensian Monks, or White Canons, and dissolved at the Reformation, when its revenues were applied by Wolsey to the erection of colleges at Ipswich and Oxford: it was afterwards forfeited to the Crown, and granted by Elizabeth to Viscount Montague, whose descendants sold it to Lord Chief Justice Pratt, grand uncle of the present marquis.

The country through which the railway passes, between Frant and Robertsbridge, a space of about fourteen miles, is very thinly populated and presents few objects requiring notice; though it must not be supposed that it is altogether wild and uncultivated; for there are great numbers of hop-grounds, fertile-looking ploughed lands and corn-fields, with extensive plantations in every direction. Near WADHURST STATION, at the fifty-second mile, is a pretty long tunnel; and five miles further is the TICEHURST-ROAD STATION, three miles beyond which again is the ETCHINGHAM STATION, fifty-nine miles from London, and thirteen from Tunbridge Wells. The village of *Ticehurst*, which is situated on an eminence about a mile and a half east of the station, is surrounded by a beautiful and diversified country, and is one of the largest in the northern part of Sussex: it comprises about 3000 inhabitants, mostly employed in agricultural pursuits. *Etchingham*, otherwise little remarkable, boasts a very fine cruciform church with a square tower and short spire or pinnacle; and it is said to be one of the best specimens of Norman architecture in this part of the country. The completion of the sixty-second mile brings us to the ROBERTSBRIDGE STATION, where the eye is attracted by a quaint-looking old village of red-brick houses, now called *Robertsbridge*, a corruption of Rotherbridge, so called from its position on the Rother: here was formerly a Cistercian Abbey, the property of which on the Dissolution was granted to Sir William Sidney. At no great distance from this part of the line are several estates, including *Iridge Place*, belonging to Sir S. Micklethwaite, Bart.; *Court Lodge*, J. Smee, Esq.; and *Darvel Bank*, B. Davenport, Esq.; but they are not seen from the carriages.

At length, at the completion of the sixty-eighth mile, the railway reaches BATTLE STATION, an extremely tasteful Gothic building—in fact, one of the prettiest built by this company—and constructed in a deep cutting, which effectually hides the town. *Battle*, as most persons know, took its present appellation from the celebrated " battle of Hastings," fought near here Oct. 14, 1066, between Harold, King of England, and William, Duke of Normandy, the result of which was to place the latter on the throne of this country. The town was formerly called St. Mary in the Wood; and though the place received its name of Battle from the engagement alluded to, the fight itself really occurred at the village of Essiton. After the battle, William caused his tent to be pitched among the dead and dying, and supped with his barons on the field. The town is almost equally famous, too, for its celebrated abbey, one of the most richly endowed and highly privileged in the kingdom, the ruins of which are still of such extent as to show the magnificence of the original structure, which must have been nearly a mile in extent. The refectory, a portion of the cloisters, and the great gate at the entrance of the quadrangle, with other buildings, are still extant, and well worthy of a visit—a portion of it being formed into the residence of Sir Godfrey Webster, Bart. The town consists of a principal street leading up to the abbey, which stands near its top. The church is a handsome structure, chiefly Norman, consisting of a nave, chancel, and aisles, having also a lofty embattled tower with a fine peal of bells. There are, also, three places of worship for Dissenters. The population of the parish is about 3500, about half of which are within the town. Petty sessions are held here; and there is a large union workhouse. In the neighbourhood are extensive gunpowder-mills.

AVIARY AT ASHFORD STATION.

HASTINGS, FROM ABOVE THE RAILWAY STATION.

A ride of four miles further brings us to the St. Leonard's Station, about seventy-three miles from London, and little more than a mile from the terminus at Hastings. *St. Leonard's,* though nearly united by houses to the older town of Hastings, has a separate local act for its government, and is to all intents and purposes distinct. It is quite a modern creation; the first plans for it having been formed by Decimus Burton, the celebrated architect, about twenty-five years ago. The plan was a bold one, and it was executed with no little spirit; for within that period there have been built a noble esplanade, extending for more than half a mile along the beach; a handsome range of buildings called the *Marina,* extending some 500 feet along the sea-front of the town, fronted with a covered colonnade of the same length, and several other terraces, as well as detached villas, together with a church, assembly-rooms, bath-houses, libraries, and two or three splendid hotels. St. Leonard's, also, possesses pleasure-grounds and other appliances for the amusement or comfort of its visitors, among whom have always been many of our distinguished nobility and wealthy aristocracy: in fact, if we except Brighton, this is beyond all question the most fashionable of our sea-bathing places on the south coast. The walk along the esplanade, which reaches almost without interruption from the Marine Parade at Hastings to the Marina of St. Leonard's, nearly a mile and a half long, and commanding fine sea views, is one of the noblest of the kind in this country.

We have now at length arrived at HASTINGS, the terminus of the branch line just described; and the engraving given of the HASTINGS STATION will fully prove to our readers that the South-Eastern Company have taken all pains to make it worthy of so important a place; for it is amply provided with every species of accommodation requisite for a very large and increasing traffic.

Hastings is a very important parliamentary and municipal borough, one of the ancient *Cinque Ports* of the realm, and a market town, locally situated at the eastern extremity of Sussex, in lat. 50° 34′ N., and long. 0° 37′ E.; and it occupies the centre of a valley, or cleft, between two lofty hills, as well as a considerable space along the sea-shore. It enjoys the advantage, also, of being sheltered from the north and north-east winds by a range of steep hills; besides which, it has a beach well adapted for bathing, and commands a glorious view of the English Channel. The Hastings of modern day, moreover, is far superior to what it was half a century ago, for then it was little better than a fishing-port, comprising two chief streets, lined with shabby-looking houses, and having many grotesque-looking tenements, belonging to the fishermen close down upon the shore. Since that time, however, the town has undergone a complete metamorphosis; many handsome new streets and squares have been formed, giving symmetry and elegance to a place that was previously irregularly built, dirty, and poverty-stricken; besides which, the beach has been vastly improved by the removal of the quaint-looking old fishing-huts that formerly so much obstructed the sea view. Among the modern improvements, we may mention more particularly *Pelham Place* and *Pelham Crescent*, the former consisting of a fine range of buildings, erected under the sandstone cliffs at the end of the Marine Parade, leading from St. Leonard's, of which, indeed, it forms the eastern extremity; while the latter comprises about sixteen noble mansions, erected on a terrace formed by arched stone buildings, which consist of shops, and a handsome arcade, converted into a bazaar. The terrace above is ascended by a handsome flight of steps, and commands a magnificent view of the sea. *Wellington Square*, also, is a very handsome feature in the modern town, and comprises a considerable number of first-class houses, built on three sides, protected from the east winds by the castle-cliff, and having the fourth side open towards the sea. These, however, are by no means the only modern buildings erected here, for in all directions rows of good houses may be seen, forming streets and terraces which had no existence thirty years ago ; in fact, few marine towns have made such extensive progress within a comparatively short period as Hastings. There are two old parish churches, neither of them very remarkable for architectural beauty, an elegant new church in Pelham Crescent, built principally at the expense of the Earl of Chichester, and a modern district church in the suburban village of Halton; all of which are well attended, and have attached Sunday-schools, besides other religious charities. Several chapels, also, give abundant accommodation to Wesleyan Methodists, Independents, Baptists, and other classes of Dissenters, who form rather an important section of the permanent population. Hastings has a very handsome town-hall, with attached offices for the transaction of municipal and magisterial business, a well-built custom-house, and a fine market-place in George-street, admirably supplied with all kinds of provisions, especially with fish, not to be excelled in any part of our southern coast. There are, also, well-appointed and extensive baths, handsome assembly-rooms, and a small theatre, open during autumn. A grammar-school and free-school, the latter conducted on the national system ; and likewise several other establishments of a similar nature, furnish abundant educational advantages; besides which, the town possesses literary and mechanics' institutes, libraries, reading-rooms, news-rooms, and other accommodations for those who prefer the *dolce-far-niente* to the more active pursuits of a business life. The old castle above the town is one of those features of our ancient historical grandeur which must ever command the attention of antiquarians, and there is still sufficient left of it to show its former importance as one of our maritime strongholds. It was built very shortly after the Norman conquest, and long maintained in a fortified state, to defend the southern coast ; but it was allowed to go into decay during the Civil wars, and has never since been repaired. Hastings, which at one time possessed many valuable privileges, as one of the principal Cinque Ports (and some of which it still retains), is governed by a mayor, five other aldermen, and eighteen councillors, and has a borough court, under a recorder. It has also sent members to the House of Commons since the reign of Edward I., its present members being P. F. Robertson and M. Brisco, Esquires. The neighbourhood of Hastings abounds with beautiful walks, both towards Battle inland and along the shore towards St. Leonard's ; besides which, there is fine exercising ground for equestrians on Fairlight Downs and onward towards Winchelsea. The lover of character, also, will find a rich treat from studying the peculiarities of the fishing population, whose fine sturdy forms, grotesque attire, quaint manners, and fond attachment to their own particular calling, stamp them as a distinct class from most others of the same vocation.

## CHAPTER VIII.

### ISLE OF THANET BRANCH.

Wye, its Manor and College—Godmersham—Chilham Castle—Canterbury, its Cathedral and Antiquities—Grove Ferry—Minster—Ramsgate and Margate— Sandwich and Deal.

HAVING thus completed our account of the Hastings branch of the South-Eastern Railway, we shall proceed to that of the Isle of Thanet branch, returning for that purpose to the junction station at Ashford (sixty-seven miles from London). The country now to be passed, as far as Canterbury, is of that beautiful and fertile character which so justly entitles this part of Kent to be called the garden of England; for orchards, hop-plantations, and corn-fields, everywhere exhibit proofs of nature's bounty. The first station on this branch is at *Wye*, which is celebrated as having once been a royal manor, and granted by the Conqueror to the Abbey of Battle, to which it belonged till the Dissolution, when it reverted to the Crown: it was subsequently granted by Queen Elizabeth to Lord Hunsdon, but at the close of the seventeenth century to the Finches, whose present representative, the Earl of Winchelsea, now possesses it. It boasted also of a monastic college, founded in the middle of the fifteenth century by John Kempe, Cardinal Archbishop of Canterbury and Lord Chancellor of England, and which was much frequented by students down to the Reformation, when it was surrendered to the Crown. The remains of it, which are sufficiently extensive to indicate its former importance, form a large quadrangle built round an open court; but though the lower part is of stone, in the pointed style of architecture, the general effect has been spoiled by modern brick additions in the upper story. The old hall, a large vaulted apartment, is now converted into a school-room, and the ancient commons-room has become a kitchen: the cloister in the inner court is modern.  Some of the windows, however, in the southern part of the college show traces of having been richly ornamented with stained glass windows marked with the arms of the founder, Edward IV. and Edward VI.  The college is still used as a grammar-school.  The town of Wye, which stands close to the River Stour (crossed here by a stone bridge), consists of a couple of well-built main streets, and has a handsome church with a fine tower that is a conspicuous object in the surrounding country.  At a short distance from it, likewise, is *Spring-grove*, a handsome seat formerly belonging to the Bretts, from whom it passed by marriage to —— Goldsmidt, Esq.; and on the banks of the Stour is *Ollantigh*, a fine mansion, surrounded by a park of about 600 acres, the property of J. Sawbridge, Esq.  On the same river, also, is *Godmersham*, a pretty rural village, in a fertile district; and close to it is Godmersham House and Park, the property of H. Galley Knight, Esq.

CHILHAM HOUSE AND CHURCH.

Six miles further, and we arrive at CHILHAM STATION, an intermediate station six miles before reaching Canterbury.  *Chilham* appears, from certain Roman remains, to have had an existence even at that early period; but we know comparatively little of it till the Conquest, when it became the property of Odo, the Conqueror's nephew. It then passed through several hands, and among others, Lord Badlesemere, of Leeds Castle; being afterwards granted, in the reign of Henry VIII., to Sir Thomas Chenewarden, of the Cinque Ports, who pulled down a large portion of the materials for the purpose of building a mansion in the Isle of Sheppy. The whole of the ancient house was demolished by his descendant, Sir Dudley Digges, who erected on its site the present magnificent edifice, completed in 1616. The modern edifice is a stately structure, and the grounds around it command an extensive and splendid view over the entire vale of Ashford and the Stour, with the fine tower of Ashford church in front, besides numerous seats, with their adjacent parks, villages, and churches, bounded southward and westward by Wye and Braborne Downs. Above the castle also, to the north-west, are the remains of its ancient Norman keep, an octagonal structure with a square building on its eastern side, containing a circular wooden staircase to the upper stories, in the third or highest of which were the principal apartments. The old doors and windows, however, with their ornaments, have wholly disappeared; and though the whole has a venerable appearance from being covered with ivy, it is impossible to form any conjecture as to its original condition. From the great extent, however, of the area enclosed by the castle-ditch—not less than eight acres—there can be no doubt that the former castle was, as Leland described it, " commodious for use,"—" beautiful for pleasure,"—and " strong for defence and resistance." The antiquarian excursionist will find his account, also, in paying a visit to the barrows and entrenchments on Chartham and Swerdling Downs; nor will he forget the pretty village of *Chartham*, close to the Stour, and its fine old cross church, one of the most elegant and best preserved in this part of Kent,—containing also some noble painted-glass windows, and several good old monuments. At no great distance, moreover, is the picturesque village of *Boughton*, surrounded by orchards and hop-plantations; close to which is *Nash Court*, the demesne of the Hawkins family since the reign of Edward III.,—an imposing mansion, situated on a height in the midst of a spacious, well-planted park, and commanding extensive views over the surrounding country.

G

## THE ECCLESIASTICAL CITY OF CANTERBURY.

BEHOLD us now rapidly approaching the world-famed city of Canterbury, the *Durwhern* of the ancient Britons, the *Durovernum* of the warlike Romans, "the chief city of Ethelbert" and the kingdom of Kent during the Heptarchy, the seat of the earliest Romish monastery in England, as well as one of the oldest and finest cathedrals in the kingdom,—a cathedral, too, of great historical interest, as having been the scene (A.D. 1170) of the murder of Thomas à Becket, an ambitious, overbearing prelate, afterwards the most fashionable saint of Roman Catholic England, to whose shrine flowed, for nearly four centuries, a continuous and abundant tide of wealth, brought by pilgrims from every part of the country.

Canterbury—which the railway approaches by its western suburb, St. Dunstan's, close to its only remaining gate, called *West-gate*, erected in the fourteenth century, by Archbishop Sudbury (and shown in our engraving)—is seated in a fertile valley about two miles wide, surrounded by hills of a moderate height, which give rise to several springs of fine water; besides which, the river Stour runs through it, dividing into many channels that form numerous islands, and turn several mills, some of which boast a high antiquity. The town was originally comprised within fortifications of an irregular octagonal shape, the remains of which still exist, and had four main streets branching from the centre, terminated by gates: but its boundaries have subsequently been much extended; and it now takes in extensive suburbs, the largest of which are eastward, on the Deal and Dover roads. The *High-street*, which is the principal avenue, upwards of half a mile long, is lined with well-built houses, and has near its centre a fine modern-built Guildhall: the other principal streets are *Stour-street, Castle-street, Mercery-lane,* and *Burgate-street,* none of them, however, possessing any very remarkable features except to the antiquarian. The present city within the walls comprises seven entire parishes, with parts of five others, besides the precincts of the *Palace* and *Christchurch* (chiefly occupied by the cathedral), *Staplegate,* and the very ancient

CANTERBURY, FROM THE LINE.

district of *St. Augustine's;* but in the suburbs are two other entire
parishes, with parts of four more—all now comprised within the municipal and electoral boundaries. The churches, though few of them
large or imposing from their architectural splendour, are perhaps more
interesting to the antiquarian than any in the kingdom—especially
*St. Dunstan's,* with its semicircular towers and fine altar-tombs,
*St. Mildred's,* at the south end of Stour-street, *St. Mary Magdalen's,*
in Burgate-street, and the fine old church of *St. Martin's,* in the
suburbs, where St. Augustine preached to the good Queen Bertha, on
his first arrival at Canterbury.

The great glory, however, of the good city of Canterbury is its cathedral, which forms a conspicuous object from every quarter of approach.
The cathedral precincts comprise an area three-quarters of a mile in
circuit, and the principal entrance is through Christchurch-gate, erected
early in the sixteenth century, which exhibits a beautiful highly ornamented specimen of later English architecture, with two octagonal

NAVE of CANTERBURY CATHEDRAL.

embattled towers flanking the archway. The present structure occupies
the site of an older one, founded by St. Augustine in connexion with

the ancient monastery of Christchurch, established by the pious mu-nificence of Ethelbert, King of Kent, after his conversion to Christianity, at the close of the sixth century; and its oldest part dates from 1184, about fourteen years after Becket's murder. The nave, cloisters, and chapter-house, however, are at least two centuries older, and were erected during the most brilliant period of pointed church-architecture. The present structure is of the usual cruciform shape, with a semi-circular east end, and 530 feet long from east to west, and 370 feet from north to south, at the intersection of the transepts: the length of the choir is 178 feet, being the largest in the kingdom, and that of the nave 214 feet; while the height of the vaulted roof is 80 feet, and that of the *Bell-Harry*, or Great Tower (one of the purest and most beauti-ful specimens of the pointed style in England), 235 feet. The nave is chiefly in the early English style, intermixed with Norman, which prevails also in the east transept; but the choir is wholly of pointed English architecture. The Archbishop's throne and the prebendal stalls are strikingly elegant; and a new stone altar has recently been erected, from designs made to correspond with the rest of the building. Beneath the church, under its whole extent, likewise, is a beautiful crypt (the largest in England), divided into two parts corresponding with those of the cathedral, and having a vaulted roof supported on pillars, which never fails to call forth the admiration of its visitors. The interior of the church, now entirely restored, is not only a work of almost matchless beauty itself, but abounds also with objects of re-markable historical interest. First of all, there is a spot pointed out on the north side of the western transept, where Becket was supposed to have been assassinated: but the only traces of his martyr-shrine are to be found in the marks on the pavement, said to have been made by the knees of the multitudinous worshippers, who flocked hither with their oblations during more than three centuries, hoping to obtain, *through his merits*, forgiveness of their sins. In fact, this turbulent canonised priest must have been held in marvellously high esteem; for we find, in a list of contributions to the principal altars of the cathedral-church for one year, that while the altar of St. Thomas à Becket re-ceived the enormous sum (for those days) of 954*l.* 6*s.*, that of the poor Virgin Mary was enriched by only 4*l.*, and that of Christ himself obtained *not even a fraction!* Scarcely, then, need we wonder that, with this tide of wealth constantly flowing into the cathedral treasury, " divine service was celebrated with a pomp and splendour almost unknown elsewhere, and that the vestry was filled with jewellery, candlesticks, cups, pixes, and crosses, of every size, made of silver and gold, many of them gorgeously and curiously adorned, with mitres and pastoral staves gemmed with costly* and rare stones," the whole amounting to many thousand pounds in value. To the north-east of the cathedral is *St. Augustine's College*, formerly a monastery, but now converted into a diocesan college, for the education of theological students. It is an extremely handsome structure, and has recently been repaired and enlarged in a style corresponding with its former grandeur.

Canterbury is a borough of great antiquity, and possesses many charters, granted by different sovereigns, from Henry III. to Charles II. It is now divided into three wards, and governed by a mayor, five other aldermen, and eighteen councillors, having also a borough-court under a recorder. It has enjoyed the privilege also of sending two representatives to Parliament since the reign of Edward I., who are still returned by registered electors under the Reform Act; but the borough has recently obtained a rather unenviable notoriety, in consequence of the bribery practised at the late election. Canterbury has large weekly corn-markets, as well as—during the season—for hops, with excellent provision markets, and an annual fair. Troops are generally quartered here, for whose accommodation there are extensive barracks; and, though it be a place of little internal trade, there are numerous genteel families living here, who, with the surrounding gentry, furnish ample business for the retail shopkeepers. Vellum and parchment, however, are made here in considerable quantities, and Canterbury brawn has obtained almost a world-wide celebrity. The population, in 1851, somewhat exceeded 8000.

The railway at this point sends off a short branch to *Sturry* and *Herne Bay*—the latter a modern-built watering-place, with a flat shore and far-projecting pier, well known to river excursionists. It has

---

* Erasmus (from whom we have taken this quotation) saw Becket's shrine before its dismantling, and in describing that prelate's shrine, says: " A coffin of wood, which covered a coffin of gold, was drawn up by ropes and pulleys, and then an invaluable treasure was described; gold was the meanest thing to be seen there; all shone and glittered with the rarest and most precious jewels of an extraordinary size—some even larger than the egg of a goose."

two good hotels, also, and an abundance of lodging-houses for summer visitors, with libraries, baths, and other conveniences; besides which, it commands a fine view of the Nore, Queen's Channel, and other approaches to the busy Thames.  The main line proceeds in an east-north-east direction, through a richly-cultivated country, and at length, eight miles from Canterbury, enters the Isle of Thanet, near the GROVE-FERRY STATION, where the line crosses the Wansum, now an insignificant stream; though about four centuries ago it was a navigable strait or creek, through which merchant vessels passed, instead of going round the North Foreland outside the island.  At this point the antiquarian-excursionist may pause awhile, to pay a visit, about four miles northward, to *Reculver*, the ancient Rutupiæ, celebrated among the Romans for its oysters, and subsequently, still more so, for its Saxon palace and church—the latter of which, with its two pyramidal towers close to the beach, merits an attentive examination.  The arch of the northern door is circular, that of the western pointed; and the chancel and altar are considerably raised above the nave by a handsome flight of steps, while over the west door is a curious triforium gallery.  Close to the church, also, are pretty extensive remains of a Roman camp or station, extending over somewhat more than eight acres; and it may possibly have been in their day as important a place as Richborough, a very similar station near Sandwich.

Proceeding five miles onward along the line we arrive at MINSTER STATION, near the village of that name, which is principally remarkable for its very handsome cross church, the nave of which is Saxon, while the chancel and transept are in the early English or pointed style; the whole is in good preservation, and comprises some good ornamental work.  The downs above the village command a splendid view from the Isle of Sheppy westward, to Deal on the east, with Canterbury Cathedral on the south, the whole bounded by a circle of hills terminating the prospect.  The manor of Thorne, in this parish, is the property of Ramsgate.  It must be remarked, also, that Minster is a junction station, whence a branch line diverges to the ancient town of Sandwich and the sea-faring town of Deal, the latter of which is 102 miles from the London Terminus and ten from Minster.  *Sandwich*, one of the Cinque Ports, had formerly a large harbour, much frequented by shipping; but this has long ago been choked up, and the place has become comparatively unimportant.  It is situated on a flat, irregularly built, and has two or three churches, with other structures, of considerable antiquity. Brewing and malting are the principal trades of this very dull town.  About four miles south-south-east is *Deal*, divided into a lower and upper town, forming an irregular continuous street along the shore, which has a bold, shingly beach, exactly facing the Downs, a well-known haven for shipping, from supplying which, indeed, the town derives its principal trade.  Deal possesses a strong castle built by Henry VIII., and inhabited by a commandant appointed by the Warden of the Cinque Ports ; besides which, in Upper Deal, there are large depôt-barracks, erected during the late war.  About a mile south, also, is *Walmer Castle*, the official residence of the Lord Warden of the Cinque Ports, in which capacity the late Duke of Wellington occupied it nearly twenty years, closing here his long and valuable life, September 14, 1852.  Though small, it is strongly fortified ; and the apartments command a splendid sea view.

Now we are at the RAMSGATE STATION (ninety-seven miles from London and sixteen from Canterbury)—a principal and very well-arranged station, with every accommodation suitable for the traffic of so important a place as *Ramsgate*, which the railway has brought within three hours' distance of the metropolis.  The town was originally built in a hollow formed by a depression of the chalk cliffs ; but since the construction of its fine pier, and its great popularity as a watering-place, the cliffs on either side have been covered with terraces, squares, crescents, and rows of houses, that furnish ample accommodation for all classes of visitors, from the luxurious *millionaire* to the humble tradesman.  The sands are excellent for bathing, and are the favourite resort, also, of a large portion of the visitors during the summer.  The chief glory of Ramsgate, however, is its splendid harbour formed by two piers, that on the east side 2000 feet, and the western 1550 feet long, leaving an opening 200 feet wide, and enclosing a water area of forty-eight acres, divided into an inner and outer harbour, the former enclosed by flood-gates and provided with a commodious graving-dock, the latter drying nearly to its entrance at low water.  At the end of the western pier is a lighthouse, where, during night, a light is exhibited when the tide permits the entrance of vessels.  The piers are built of granite and Purbeck stone, rising fifteen

RAMSGATE, FROM THE HARBOUR.

feet above high-water mark, and are twenty-six feet broad at top, furnishing a beautiful and airy promenade to the inhabitants and visitors. The harbour-master has a handsome residence close to the gates at the eastern entrance, the western pier being approached by the wall dividing the two basins, as well as from the cliff above by a staircase, familiarly known as *Jacob's-ladder*. The port is accessible to vessels not exceeding 400 tons burden within two hours of high water, and, owing to its safety, is annually visited by about 1500 ships; besides which, it enjoys a small trade with Holland and the Baltic, and a considerable coasting trade. Its marine population, too, are extensively engaged in fishing and going to the aid of vessels in distress on the Goodwin Sands, directly opposite, at a distance of five or six miles. Ramsgate has a handsome parish church, a district church, chapel of ease, and places of worship for Independents, Baptists, and Wesleyan Methodists, besides a Jew's synagogue. The streets, also, are well paved or macadamised, and brilliantly lighted with gas; but the town is very inadequately supplied with water of a harsh, bad quality. Ramsgate has two banking establishments and a savings bank, with a literary institute, assembly-rooms, a small theatre, two or three good libraries, and other appliances for instruction and amusement. The bathing-machines are under the East Cliff, where also, as well as in front of the harbour, there are well-appointed warm baths, &c.; but the most complete establishment of this kind is on the West Cliff, situated 125 feet above high water, and supplied by pumps from the sea: it comprises cold and warm sea-water baths, vapour and douche baths, &c., and has a well-supplied news-room. The markets are extremely well supplied with meat, excellent fish, &c.; and few places on the coast are so cheap, as well as healthy and agreeable for a summer's residence. Neither must we omit to notice the numerous pretty walks and drives in the neighbourhood; to *Pegwell Bay*, noted for its fish-dinners and shrimp-teas, westward; or along the cliffs, eastward, to the retired *Broadstairs*; or more inland, to *St. Lawrence's* and *St. Peter's;* or, further still, to *Birchington*, or the *North Foreland Lighthouse* : in fact, the visitor here need never be at a loss for pretty scenery and healthful exercise, whether he seeks it by land or sea; those who prefer the latter having ample opportunities of sailing in vessels daily taking company to the Downs, Deal, Dover, &c.

MARGATE, FROM THE RAILWAY STATION.

We shall now proceed onwards, and take a further run of four miles to the MARGATE TERMINUS, for the purpose of visiting Margate, long celebrated as the marine paradise of cockney invalids and health-seekers. The older town is built on the shore close to the port, and on the acclivity rising south-west therefrom; but since this watering-place has been so much frequented by summer visitors, extensive additions have been made both on the cliffs eastward and along the shore towards the west, especially the latter. Although, therefore, Margate may not boast of so high a class of company as it did in the palmy days of Hawley-square and Betterson's, forty years ago, the vast numbers who yearly flock thither now contribute far more to the prosperity of the town. There are two handsome churches, and several places of worship for Dissenters, with attached schools, providing religious instruction for about 1800 children; the other public buildings being the assembly-rooms, theatre, market-house, and leading hotels. The chief feature of Margate, however, is its handsome stone pier, the upper terrace of which forms a favourite promenade for visitors. It was planned by the elder Rennie, and consists of a double platform, one for landing passengers from steamers, goods from vessels, &c., while the other is railed, and handsomely flagged for the accommodation of such as love to inhale the sea breeze and gaze on the fine sea view that it commands. It projects nearly 1000 feet from the shore, and has a handsome lighthouse at its further extremity, the light from which indicates at night when the harbour is accessible; for it cannot be entered, even by the London steamers, except when it is more than half-tide. It was this circumstance, indeed, which led to the construction of the jetty (often called, from the person who suggested it, *Jarvis's Landing Place*), and here the steamers land their passengers at such times as the pier-head cannot be approached. It is an extensive timber platform, projecting several hundred feet into the sea, at the back or east side of the pier, and so openly constructed, that while it offers little or no resistance to the rising tide, it furnishes a safe landing from vessels, and an agreeable lounge or promenade at those times when it is left uncovered by water. This is a very favourite resort for the summer visitors of all classes and ages, from the hobbling valetudinarian to the romping child; and most amusing are the scenes and incidents that may often be witnessed here, forming most agreeable, as well as instructive lessons on the habits and idiosyncracies of London's out-for-a holiday population. The bathing at Margate, though perhaps inferior to that of Ramsgate, is still, on the whole, very good; and there are waiting-rooms, with papers, books, pianos, and other appliances for allaying the impatience of bathers abiding their time for using the machines, which are well conducted under the superintendence of experienced attendants. Margate has, also, some excellent warm baths—the establishment on the East Cliff, in particular, being admirably adapted to the requirements of invalids. About a mile westward, too, close on the beach, is the Margate Sea-bathing Infirmary. As respects amusements, there are numerous bazaars, lounges, news-rooms, libraries, &c., where the visitor may very agreeably while away the lagging hours, and often listen to very tolerable music and singing by professionals engaged from London; while for those who prefer *al fresco* amusement, there is a mimic Vauxhall, called the *Tivoli*, outside the town, where singing, dancing, fireworks, &c., furnish ample means of delectation to those who love the coarser kinds of merriment. Those, also, who are fond of walking or riding exercise, may indulge therein to their heart's content by making excursions to *Dandelion*, where there are pretty pleasure-gardens, to *Reculver's* ancient ruins, to the villages of *Monckton* and *Minster*, and the retired village of *Kingsgate*, once remarkable for some grotesque ruins, erected with execrable taste by Lord Holland, the father of C. J. Fox the celebrated statesman; besides which, *Broadstairs* and *Ramsgate* are so near, as to be within the limits of a pleasant walk. In fact, the visitor of this very popular watering-place will not lack amusement and occupation while he is seeking health and vigour from the fine breezes and sea-bathing which it furnishes in such perfection. The town, it may be remarked, in conclusion, is exceedingly well-regulated by commissioners, and is well-paved, lighted with gas, and adequately supplied with water. Two or three steamers daily run to and from London, and during the summer there are numerous excursion trips; but the facilities for communication with the metropolis have within the last few years greatly increased by the South-Eastern Railway Company, who send thither six trains daily, performing the journey in three or four hours—about half the time occupied by the steamers.

# CHAPTER IX.

## REIGATE AND READING BRANCH.

Betchworth—Box Hill and Norbury Park—DORKING, Deepdene, and Denby's—
Shere and Albury—Chilworth and Shalford—GUILDFORD and its Ancient Castle
—Ash and Farnborough—Blackwater and Sandhurst—Wokingham—READING.

THIS important branch line, which connects the main line of the
South-Eastern with the Great Western, at Reading, is altogether forty-
five miles in length, and passes through a fine country, dotted with
country-seats and pretty villages, having principal stations, also, at the
important towns of Dorking, Guildford, and Wokingham. The first
portion of it skirts the southern slope of a well-known range of hills,
called the *North Downs*, but diverges somewhat southward, as it passes
Shere and Chilworth on its way to Guildford. The high ground of Box
Hill is tunnelled through, and the little sluggish river Mole is crossed
by a handsome viaduct of five arches, elevated fifty feet above the
stream ; but besides these the railway in this part presents no peculiar
features, beyond the alternation of short deep cuttings and moderately
high embankments. The BETCHWORTH STATION, near the very pretty village of that name, is three miles from Reigate ; and not far from it are the
handsome demesnes of *Betchworth House*, belonging to the Right Hon.
Henry Goulburn, M.P., and *Broome Park*, the property of Sir Benjamin
Brodie, Bart., the celebrated surgeon. A mile and a half further,
through the tunnel, and we have reached the BOX HILL STATION, a
small intermediate one, at no great distance from *Burford Bridge*,
where is a pretty rural hostelrie, much frequented in summer by
visitors to Box Hill and its beautiful scenery. The beauties of this
neighbourhood, indeed, require a description of themselves ; but we may
just mention that the summit of this well-known hill commands a fine
view of the country for many miles round, including *Norbury Park*, the
property of Thomas Grissell, Esq., in the foreground, with the pretty
village of Mickleham.

Six miles from Reigate, and twenty-nine (by railway) from London, the railway reaches the DORKING STATION, on the north-western side of the market town so called, which we must now very briefly describe.

DORKING, FROM THE LINE.

It is situated in a sandy valley, on the south bank of the Mole, and consists of a wide and handsome principal street, with two others branching out at its southern end, the whole town being very clean, well-paved, and lighted with gas. It has a handsome church, with a tower and spire, rebuilt in 1837, and containing a fine mausoleum belonging to the Duke of Norfolk, the lord of the manor; besides which there are district churches at Holmwood Common and Westcott, near Bury Hill, the seat of C. Barclay, Esq. There are places of worship, also, for Wesleyan Methodists, Independents, and the Society of Friends, with national and infant schools. Dorking, celebrated for its breed of fowls, has a large weekly market for corn, poultry, &c., and monthly cattle markets; with a pretty extensive trade in corn, flour, and lime obtained from the neighbouring chalk hills. It is also one of the polling places for West Surrey, a place for holding petty-sessions, and the central town of a large union, the workhouse of which is in the outskirts.   The neighbourhood, moreover, is adorned with some very beautiful country seats ; among which we may notice *Shrub Hill*, belonging to Lady E. Wathen ; *Deepdene*, a fine Italian villa, surrounded by beautiful grounds, which its present owner, H. T. Hope, Esq., has greatly extended by throwing into them the estates of Betchworth and Chart parks ; and *Denby's*, on an elevation about two miles north-west, the mansion of which was built, in 1734, by Jonathan Tyers, the originator of Vauxhall ; this estate now belongs to Thomas Cubitt, Esq., the celebrated engineer.   About three miles south is *Wootton*, long the abode of George Evelyn, the author of the " Sylva ;" and about a mile beyond is *Leith Hill*, 993 feet high, the most elevated spot in Surrey, commanding a view of London northward, and of the British Channel to the south.

A ride of five miles further brings us to the GOMSHALL and SHERE STATION, a small intermediate station, close to the retired village of Shere, and not far from *Albury Park*, the residence of H. Drummond, Esq., M.P. for West Surrey, who has erected a new church for the parish of Albury.   Close to the village, also, lives Martin F. Tupper, Esq., the celebrated poet.   Four miles further, and we reach CHILWORTH STATION (seventeen miles from Reigate), near which may be seen St. Martha's ancient chapelry, on a considerable elevation to the south.   *Chilworth Manor* belongs to R. A. Austin, Esq.   Two miles more, and we are at SHALFORD STATION, about half a mile from the pretty village of that name on the Wey, near which is *Shalford House*, the fine demesne of Sir Henry Austin, whose mansion contains some good carved work, and a choice collection of pictures by the old masters.   A little northward is the village of *Merrow*, and on a height to the south-west may be seen the picturesque ruins of *St. Catherine's Hill*.

We have now arrived at the GUILDFORD STATION, a principal and very important one (nineteen miles from Reigate and thirteen from Dorking), having all the conveniences for the traffic of a large and populous county-town.   Guildford is imposingly seated on the declivity of a steep hill rising from the eastern bank of the Wey (crossed here by a modern iron bridge) ; and it consists of a good principal street, mostly lined with well-built houses, and running nearly a mile from north-east to south-west, being joined at its lower extremity by the continuous suburb

GUILDFORD CASTLE, &C.

H

of Stoke; besides which there are several smaller streets, parallel to or running out of the main thoroughfare. In speaking of the public buildings, the first place is due to the ancient *Castle*, built most probably in Saxon times; and although its quadrangular keep is nearly all that now remains, standing boldly on the brow of the hill facing the west, and constructed chiefly of ragstone, flint, and chalk, there are traces of foundations that prove the original building to have covered altogether more than four acres of ground. The tower consists of three stories; but all the floors, together with the roof itself, have long been destroyed, and there is no access to the upper part, except by steps or ladders. There are some crypts, also, once forming a part of the castle, that are well worthy of examination. On the north side of the High-street is the *Guildhall*, a large brick building, surmounted by an open turret, with a projecting clock in front, and containing a council-chamber, and a hall for the assizes, quarter-sessions, county and borough courts, &c. Immediately opposite is a handsome modern building with a lofty portico, the Corn-market House, where the corn-markets are held twice a week; besides which there is a large vegetable market-house in Market-street, and a new market for poultry, butter, &c. Near the top of High-street, too, is Abbot's Hospital, a substantial red-brick building, fronted by a square tower with octagonal turrets surmounting a spacious archway:—it was founded by Archbishop Abbot, early in the seventeenth century, for the residence and support of a master, twelve brethren, and eight sisters, upwards of sixty years old and unmarried. Parson's Hospital, for the support of poor widows, is in the suburb of Stoke. Guildford has likewise a well-endowed grammar-school, a blue-coat school, another charity-school, two national schools, a British and an infant school, with several money-charities. The town is divided into three parishes, two on the east and the third on the west side of the Wey. Trinity church is a large red-brick structure, with a high square tower near the top of the town, and contains a fine altar-tomb of Archbishop Abbot. St. Mary's is an ancient rudely-built edifice on the declivity of the hill, with two semicircular chapels and a low embattled tower, the whole well worthy of inspection for its curious monuments; and St. Nicholas is a handsome fabric, in the pointed style, with a square tower, near the bridge at the bottom of the town. Guildford has places of worship, also, for Independents, Baptists, Wesleyan-Methodists, and the Society of Friends, to all or most of which there are attached Sunday-schools. The other public buildings are the county-gaol and house of correction, a large modern red-brick structure; an union workhouse; a small theatre; and a lofty prospect tower, near the gas-works, called Booker's Tower. The town possesses, besides, a well-supported literary and scientific institution, a mechanics' institute, agricultural and horticultural societies, and two banking establishments. It has been incorporated since the reign of Edward I., and is now governed by a mayor, three other aldermen, and twelve councillors, with a recorder; besides which it is a parliamentary borough, having for its present members R. D. Mangles and James Bell, Esquires. It is the place of election, also, for West Surrey, and the centre of a large poor-law union. The town has a considerable business in curing bacon, and a large trade in corn, malt, timber, &c., with two annual fairs.

Six miles beyond Guildford is the Ash Station, a small intermediate one, near the long-scattered village of that name, not far from which are *Henley Park*, belonging to H. Halsey, Esq., and *Ash Lodge*, the residence of Mrs. Bree. Here the line turns more to the north; and another stage of four miles brings us to Farnborough, where the line is intersected by the South-Western Railway, and where, therefore, there is a considerable junction station. Near it is Farnborough Hill, the property of the Dean of Chichester. The road soon afterwards enters the valley of the Blackwater, which it crosses by a skew-bridge, and twenty-nine miles from Reigate reaches the Blackwater Station, near the small village of that name, and not far from *Heron Court*, the noble demesne of the Earl of Malmesbury. At Sandhurst, too, a mile further, is another small intermediate station, constructed to accommodate the students of *Sandhurst Military College*, situated a little to the right of the line in the centre of a spacious park; this institution was founded by the late Duke of York for the scientific education of cadets and junior commissioned officers, and it is well conducted under the superintendence of a governor (Sir George Scovell), a lieutenant-governor (Major-General T. W. Taylor), and a large staff of instructors.

The railroad now pursues a pretty straight course north-north-west, and thirty-eight miles from Reigate reaches the WOKINGHAM STATION, a large and principal one, suitable to the wants of the large market-town, near which it passes. *Wokingham*, or *Oakingham*, is pleasantly situated on the borders of Windsor Forest, and consists of three leading streets, with an old town-hall and market-house near its centre. It has an old church, with some good monuments, and two places of worship for Dissenters, with national, British, and infant schools. There are weekly corn and poultry markets, and two annual fairs. Near the town are *Bearwood Park*, the seat of John Walter, Esq., M.P., of the *Times* newspaper, and *Arborfield Hall*, belonging to Sir John Conroy. The village of Arborfield, too, is the residence of Miss Mitford, and the scene of most of the tales in "Our Village." The country through which the line now passes is tolerably level and highly cultivated, interspersed with villages and handsome seats; and this continues to the READING TERMINUS, which it reaches after crossing the Kennet by a lofty bridge of a single arch, thirty-five miles from Reigate and twenty-six from Guildford. *Reading* is well known (and fully described in "George Measom's Illustrated Guide to the Great Western Railway") as the capital town of Berkshire, and has many architectural features that make it highly interesting to the antiquarian —as its fine old abbey, its churches, and other remains. It contains, also, a celebrated grammar-school, a large and new gaol, a public hall, literary and mechanics' institutes, &c. It is also a corporate-town, governed by a mayor, five other aldermen, and eighteen councillors, having a borough-court under a recorder; besides, it has enjoyed the privilege since 1295 of sending two representatives to Parliament—its present members being F. Pigott and H. S. Keating, Esquires. The neighbourhood, too, abounds with fine mansions and beautiful parks.

And here, courteous reader, our self-imposed task is brought to a close. If you have found in the perusal of these pages a tithe of the pleasure we have experienced in writing them, we shall be more than repaid.

THE END.

# APPENDIX.



To those of our friends who are not well acquainted with the pleasures of the metropolis, and require some Guide to those places of amusement that are most worthy of a visit, we address a few remarks on the pleasures offered at some of its leading places of entertainment.

First, then, leaving to others of more musical and exotic taste the pleasures of the Philharmonic, Ancient Concerts, &c., we shall briefly advert to the Italian Opera and National Theatres.

The ROYAL ITALIAN OPERA, COVENT GARDEN (under the talented management of Mr. Gye), is now without a competitor, its more ancient rival in the Haymarket having ceased to exist. Here may be witnessed the great *chefs d'œuvres* of Mozart, Rossini, Auber, and the mighty composers of modern day, represented by all the combined talent of the operatic world, including Mesdames Grisi, Castellan, Medori, Jullienne, Albini, Bosio, &c., Signori Mario, Tamberlik, Ronconi, Belletti, Formes, Zelzer, Tagliafico, and other celebrities, forming an unrivalled *troupe*—the finest, by far the finest company ever gathered together in one theatre—truly, the palmy days of the opera have returned—besides a large and talented *corps de ballet*, and a most magnificent orchestra, under the direction of Costa.

The HAYMARKET has recently come into the hands of Mr. Buckstone, and under his government promises to equal at least anything that has been done by former lessees. Of course, as all the world knows, he is a very host in himself as respects fun and waggery; besides which, in his late " Trip to Parnassus," in search of novelty wherewith to amuse the laughter-loving public, he has collected round him a numerous corps of talented coadjutors, including Messrs. Compton, the younger Farren, Barry Sullivan, Tilbury, Chippendale, &c., with the inimitable Mrs. Fitzwilliam, Miss Reynolds, Miss A. Vining, Louisa Howard, Mrs. Caulfield, and Miss Helen Faucit—the Helen Faucit; so being well supported by dramatic talent—if he can only procure a similar amount of talent in his authors—and who knows better how to discern it?—his undertaking must meet with the success his efforts merit. No theatre in London is visited by company so respectable and select, or less intruded on by those improper characters too commonly admitted to our metropolitan theatres.

The PRINCESS's THEATRE, under the management of Mr. Charles Kean, the great reviver of the true Shakspearian drama, is another place of dramatic entertainment, which should by all means be visited; and truly he has an excellent company—including, besides his talented wife and himself, such actors as James Vining, Walter Lacy, Graham, Ryder, F. Cooke, and the laughter-kindling Wright, with Mrs. W. Daly, Miss Le Clercq, Miss Heath, &c.   His highly classical revival of "Macbeth" is, above all others of his efforts, well worthy to be witnessed, and does Mr. Kean quite as much credit as his production of "King John" last season.   Mr. Simpson's adaptation of Scribe's drama of "Marco Spada," moreover, does immense credit to the management, and in all respects equal—as regards scenic effect—to the "Corsican Brothers," which proved so decided a hit last year.   No London theatre, in fact, is more admirably managed, or are their appointments of dress, scenery, or decoration, superior to those that are to be found in this elegant temple of Thalia.

The ADELPHI, so long under the management of Madame Celeste and Mr. Benjamin Webster, the former lessee of the Haymarket, has ever been distinguished for its highly successful representations of broad, funny farces, and stirring, well-presented melodramas; nor does it seem probable that its attractions will be diminished under the new *régime*, for the *Adelphi fare* presented and promised is of a very high character and great gusto, served up, too, by artists of consummate judgment.   Webster himself and Madame Celeste would of themselves ensure success to any series of pieces; but then we have in addition the funny little Keeley and his *naïve* harlequin-talented wife, glorious old Paul Bedford and his nephew Henry, the clever Alfred Wigan and his wife, the gruff O. Smith, Parselle, G. Honey, Rogers, Cullenford, the talented Leigh Murray, Flexmore the wonderful, Madame Auriol, pretty Miss Honey, the charming Mary Keeley, and—though last, not least—clever Miss Woolgar, the life and soul of light comedy.   "The Merry Wives of Windsor" introduces the company to the audience in a most effective manner; and the "Pretty Girls of Stilberg," with "Masks and Faces," and "A Desperate Game," are of themselves quite sufficient to render this theatre a very popular place of entertainment.

To those who love monologue entertainments  we confidently recommend a visit to ALBERT SMITH'S ASCENT OF MONT BLANC; for perhaps there is no actor in London who possesses so much versatility of talent, such happy powers of illustration, and so much true comic humour, united, also, with no small share of musical accomplishment. In combination, too, with the comic part of the business, he contrives to introduce in a playful way no small amount of information respecting the countries through which he is supposed to pass. Add to this the admirable scenic illustrations with which his amusing work is embellished, and we think none of our readers will think the two hours mis-spent which they have passed in the pleasant company of Mr. Albert Smith.

MADAME TUSSAUD'S WAX-WORK EXHIBITION (the oldest in the world), in Baker-street, specially under Royal patronage, is extremely well worthy of a visit; and many will not be content with one only; for it comprises so extensive a collection of celebrities of every age and country, from Louis Napoleon, Queen Victoria, the late Louis Philippe, and the Iron Duke, down to O'Connell, Cobbett, Fieschi, Hare, and other characters, either of fair fame or unhappy notoriety, that it may be termed quite a museum of morals. The costumes, also, are most scrupulously attended to, and the life-like resemblances are so striking, that the spectator may almost imagine himself in the company of the parties whose effigies are presented to his wondering view. An excellent band of music, too, gives further zest to the entertainment; and for those who are fond of looking on the monsters of society and their sanguinary deeds, there is the " Chamber of Horrors," where they can sup full of them to their very heart's content. On no account, therefore, should the country and foreign visitor forget to visit Madame Tussaud's, which is fully worth thrice the moderate shilling demanded for admission.

Here also, on the basement, will be found a large and magnificent collection of vases, antiquities, and Chinese produ ctions; the whole forming the West End branch of Hewett's great establishment.

THE ZOOLOGICAL GARDENS, in the Regent's Park, have long been famed for their noble collection of animals; and not a month elapses without fresh additions to this already large menagerie, which is now superior to that of the *Jardin des Plantes*, in Paris, and probably contains as many species as all the collections on the Continent put together. The animals—whether mammals, birds, or reptiles—are here seen to great perfection, especial care being taken in all instances to give them facilities, as far as possible, for the indulgence of their native habits. The hippopotamus, the rhinoceros, and several elephants, are here to be seen in great perfection; and the collection of carnivorous animals is unequalled by any in the world. The immense variety of monkeys, lemurs, &c., is truly astonishing; and there are many very splendid specimens of foreign deer and oxen. Of birds, raptorial, wading, web-footed, and insessorial, including cage-birds, their name is legion; and there are some extremely curious specimens of rare Australian animals, such as the *Tasmanian wolf*, red kangaroo, bower bird, and brush turkey, &c. Alligators, lizards, and snakes, have all of them their representatives; and the *Pythons*, or great constricting serpents, have a spacious saloon, enclosed by plate-glass, entirely devoted to them. All the animals, moreover, wherever placed, are invariably designated by labels, so that the spectator has no trouble in recognising them, and tracing the notices relating to them in the catalogue. The gardens, besides, are beautifully laid out, and kept with a care not to be surpassed in any nobleman's grounds; so that, even were the collection less extensive or rare than it really is, the place would still be fully worth a visit. We know of no exhibition in the metropolis, in fact, where a long morning can be so well or so instructively spent as in these gardens; truly the public are indebted to Mr. Mitchell. Nor must we forget to mention the Zoological Museum in the North Gardens, which contains a very instructive series of those forms which are not found living in the menagerie.

We are well aware that our modern Babylon offers many other attractions for visitors besides those already mentioned, and which, with a little experience, they will find out for themselves; but we have mentioned some of the principal, which, having seen and admired them ourselves, we can most confidently recommend to others, as worthy of their first attention.

Our gentlemen-friends will doubtless feel desirous of knowing where a really good cigar may be procured. A good foreign—really foreign —cigar, however, is by no means so easy of purchase; and it may not be amiss if we recommend from experience BENSON'S, in OXFORD-STREET, a very extensive depôt; but, *entre nous*, not in the carriages; there study our Guide, learn patriotism from THE *True Briton*, glance at the cynic *Diogenes*, or ramble over the pages of the genuine *Home Companion*.